Faces of the Tsunami

Bill McDaniel, M.D.

First edition:

ISBN: **978-1500172565**

FOTS - 8

We invite you to visit our web site:

www.FacesOfTheTsunami.com

Dedication

This book is dedicated to those countless volunteers who are really the backbone of America. To those who show up after every disaster, whether manmade or natural, bearing food, clothing, money, or just show up with the tools of their trade, ready to go to work and help their neighbors.

It is so incredibly gratifying to see this same spirit of giving repeated all over the world in similar circumstances. And, while people from all over the world show up and give the same wonderful giving effort to help, invariably Americans are everywhere giving what they can.

Following tsunamis in Indonesia and Japan, earthquakes in Haiti and China, tornadoes in Oklahoma, hurricanes on the entire Eastern seaboard, and disasters promulgated by our own, like Sandy Hook, the outpouring of help, support, money, goods, and most of all, love, from our own citizens (and businesses) somehow allow and encourage the afflicted people to carry on, to start again. And again.

So, here's to you, volunteers.

You are special people.

Bill McDaniel, MD

Faces of The Tsunami

Before and after pictures

Foreword

I WAS SITTING in a Rotary meeting on 5 Jan 2005 when my phone rang, immediately costing me a few dollars fine paid to Rotary charitable causes. I answered.

My wife was on the phone. She had just received a phone call from the #2 Admiral for the Navy in Hawaii. They were requesting that I immediately come there and work with them on the tsunami relief effort we had undertaken as a Nation a few days before.

She said she had assured the Admiral that I would certainly be happy to accept this request. I asked her how she knew that with certainty? She laughed and pointed out to me that of all the jobs I had undertaken since retiring from the Navy, none had been for the love of the job; they were just another way to make some money. She felt that finally I might have found an opportunity that I could undertake with enthusiasm. The only tasks I had undertaken since retiring with great delight and enthusiasm were hiking the Appalachian Trail and doing a reality show, "The Mole."

She was right, of course. She usually is. I would have paid them for the honor of again working for the Navy, and for helping in something this big, this worthwhile.

- - - - - - - -

ALL OUR DAYS in this Herculean effort were difficult, and all were emotional. Perhaps my emotions reached their peak one day more than two months into our venture. Truly, I look back through a blur of emotion and not a few tears, and picking one day that stands out seems nigh on to impossible. But, it might have been one day on Nias Island. We had already been in Banda Aceh for two months, and had transitioned to Nias Island after their 8.7 earthquake on 28 March 2005.

I was making rounds in the largely destroyed Gunungsitoli Hospital when they asked me if they could send a thirteen month old boy to Mercy. He had severe pneumonia, and a weeping father standing meekly by as they tried to help the infant. That boy was his only surviving family member; all the others had perished when their home collapsed during the quake. I returned to Mercy about every 3rd day to

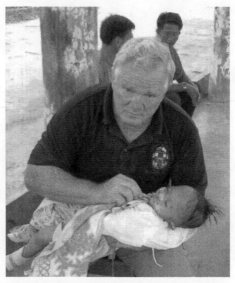

Rear Admiral Bill McDaniel Begging Benny to live

take a shower, change clothes, and get an American meal anyway, so I told them I would deliver the infant to the ship. I'm an orthopedic surgeon, and thus not entirely comfortable dealing with the severely ill, and poorly equipped to do so. Give me a broken bone and I'm happy. A baby barely breathing and gasping for breath is not exactly my forte, and indeed scares me about as much as it scares most anyone.

However, not knowing exactly what I did not know, I gathered the gravely ill infant up in my arms, with Dad holding an IV bag which was trying to deliver fluid to the severely dehydrated child through a precariously placed tiny needle in a tinier vein. I got a van to take us to the local soccer field, the staging area for our helicopters as they arrived from Mercy.

During the fifteen minute trip from the hospital to the field I noted with some alarm that the infant was really having difficulty breathing. His father had noted that fact also, and just wept harder as we rode along, sure that his son was dying. It seems that Dad was a considerably better diagnostician than I was.

Once at the field I requested the military radio operator to contact the ship and get a helo en route to us. He turned to the radio and initiated a conversation. Content with the efficiency of the communication process, I retreated under a roof shelter with the baby and his father, with an interested mix of locals looking on. They enjoyed the spectacle of the helicopters arriving and leaving, and perhaps the drama encountered occasionally when a patient was particularly ill. I was not to disappoint them.

The baby would cease breathing and start turning blue. I would shake him, wipe his face and body down with a towel, and repeatedly entreat him to breathe. The baby would gasp for a while, and then the cycle would repeat itself. I had borrowed a towel from the van that brought us to the field, and had the father keep it damp with a bottle of drinking water he had with him. Dad just wept, and the surrounding crowd watched curiously. They didn't understand anything I was saying, which was just as well; it was not medical or scientific talk at all; just abject begging for the child to live, and to continue breathing. The crowd grew to perhaps a hundred folks, watching silently. They had seen so much death that this was just another to them, I suppose. Not to me, though. I have not had a baby die in my arms...ever. I sure as hell did not want this to be the first time.

After thirty minutes or so I grew restive. The helo drivers usually responded quickly, and there was still no sign of an incoming bird. I walked over to the comms fellows and asked them if they had gotten through to the ship. Yep, they had. Father followed me along, holding the IV bag. I noted that it was not running; the IV had become dislodged and the child was no longer getting fluids. I did not have another IV set-up to attempt another stick, which I guess was a good thing. I could never have found a vein in this critically ill infant anyway.

Another thirty minutes or so passed. Now, you should understand that these were absolutely the longest minutes I had ever endured. Ever. I was constantly stimulating the child, tickling his feet, bathing him in cool water. Anything to keep him responding

9

enough to just take another breath. And another. And, I talked. Dr. Dana Braner, a wonderful pediatric intensive specialist from Portland, had told me a few days earlier when we were rescuing another very sick infant from the Russian tent hospital that he had never lost an infant while he had been talking to them. I don't know why that might be so; perhaps the babies stay alive to see what inane thing you might be saying next? Regardless, with little medical expertise to fall back on in the current circumstance, I followed Dana's advice. I talked nonstop for close to two hours. I sure hope the Indonesian onlookers did not speak English; my abject begging would not have comforted them with the tremendous knowledge base of medical care made in America!

After the longest hour's wait in my history of ill infants, I went back over to the comms guys. They assured me that they had passed the word along. I grabbed the mike from them.

"Where the hell is my helicopter?! This baby is dying here!"

There was a moment's silence. "Who is this?" the speaker responded.

"This is Admiral McDaniel! Who the hell did you think was waiting out here for you guys to show up?"

"Admiral McDaniel? Did you want a medevac chopper?"

I almost dropped the mike. "Hell, yes, I want one. I wanted one an hour ago! This kid is going to die here with Dad and about one-hundred Indonesians watching our lack of efficiency!"

Suddenly another voice came on the line. "Admiral, this the flight deck on Mercy. I'm sorry, sir, we did not get the word that you had an urgent mission; we were going to send in a routine bird later. They are departing the deck now, sir."

I don't know what happened. I know the kids at the field communication station had passed the word along; just garbled comms, I guess. As it turned out the ship was about eighty miles away, so it took another forty five for the helo to get there. It did so with style, however. Instead of the usual high slow approach so they would not disturb any of the surrounding buildings they came in low and extremely fast, blowing several sheets of tin off roofs en route.

10

Dad and I ran toward the field and were aboard within seconds of their arrival. We departed just as they had arrived, low and fast, to the cheers of the gathered onlookers. This was a far more exciting extraction than they were used to seeing out of the field. Plus, maybe they had understood the gravity of the situation. Or, perhaps they were just tired of hearing me talk. I was getting hoarse by that point. To my good fortune another physician had shown up shortly before the helo arrived, and he joined me in my efforts to keep this kid among the living. And, frankly, both of us were slowly losing ground in that effort.

We arrived back at the ship, and my friend Dr. Braner was waiting on the flight deck. (As I sit editing this for the umpteenth time, remembering my feelings when I saw an extremely competent Dana Braner waiting on the flight deck again brings me close to tears. The relief of being able to pass this kid along to someone as wonderful as Dana was at saving kids was absolutely indescribable.) Within moments he had the child back in the receiving medical ward where a gang of professionals started working on him. IV's, intubation, chest tube, etc. All the things I could not do for him on a soccer field. (or, anyplace else.) I stood, silently, watching as they swarmed around the child, feverishly working on him. The head nurse appeared next to me, clutching my arm.

"Admiral McDaniel, would you like to sit down? Can I get you something to drink?" I looked at her through a haze of tears. I was suddenly so exhausted that I was almost falling down. But, I could not leave that spot until I knew what was going to happen to the child. I tried to say something to her, but I was all talked out, I guess. I just shook my head and turned back to the action, watching. Not even hoping. I was just too tired to hope.

After some time, thirty minutes or so, my friend Dana Braner turned to me and smiled, giving me a gloved thumbs up. I turned and slowly made my way back across the ward to the chairs where Dad was sitting, still silently crying. Think about it. This slight, forty year old man had awakened six days before with his house fallen down around him, with all the members of his family dead around him. Only this one son, Benny, was alive. He was all that there was left, and he then watched him get progressively more ill with pneumonia…probably the after effects of breathing the dense dust which had arisen in the air after the earthquake. So, yep, he was still crying. Perhaps he had not stopped in six days.

I collapsed next to him, totally and completely emotionally and physically exhausted. One of the interpreters was standing near; he tapped me on the shoulder.

"Dr. McDaniel, the father wants to know if his son has died."

I felt like an idiot. I don't know why, but I guess I had assumed that he knew the team had given me a thumb's up. So, I had let him suffer a few minutes longer than he needed to.

"Tell him Benny is alive. And, I think he will live."

The interpreter chatted with the father for a few minutes. The father turned to me, eyes red and exhausted looking. I smiled and gave him a thumb's up.

"The father wants to know if he can see his son."

So I took him by the hand and led him across the medical spaces, suddenly aware of how foreign and scary this entire set-up probably was to him. When we arrived at the low retaining wall short of the bed all we could see were the backs of doctors and nurses, with the wheezing of the respirator and bags of fluid hanging from poles. Benny was totally obscured. I yelled at Dana.

"Dana, is there any chance Dad can see that his son is under all that equipment?" Dana looked up and grinned, moving a couple of people aside and revealing Benny, small and silent…but, breathing. Breathing most of all.

Dad must have had an inexhaustible source of tears, because he turned and grabbed my hand with both of his, tears again streaming down his face. With great dignity he bowed his head, touched his hand to his heart, and murmured, "Terima casi, terima casi." Thank you, thank you. Geez. All I could do was try to match him tear for tear.

I've thought about Benny many times over the years since then. I imagine he will someday have such bad dreams he will have to see a psychiatrist. His complaint will likely be that he continues to see in his dreams this big ugly freckled man leaning over him, and the guy would just not shut up. Just wouldn't shut up, like that was the most important thing he could do. Talk.

The chief nurse finally came over to me and led me away to a hot cup of coffee. I went happily, but totally depleted. I slept soundly that night.

Benny lived.

If I ever have to do something like that again, I may not.

Devastation of Banda Aceh

Chapter 1

BEING PART OF the international response to the massive earthquake and tsunami that struck Indonesia in late 2004 turned out to be a far more emotional and traumatic experience than most of us were prepared to deal with effectively, though we did not realize it until later.   But, God knows, none of our rough days began to compare to the days those phenomenal folks we were dealing with had experienced. They were the survivors of the killer tsunami that had struck Indonesia and other Indian Ocean littoral countries on 26 December 2004; most of the patients we saw were from Banda Aceh, Sumatra…a city that had suffered an absolutely horrendous death toll from the 9.3 (9.1 to 9.3; the experts are not sure) earthquake centered 135 miles away, with the subsequent massive tsunami waves that struck the city some thirty-three minutes later.

We were the military and civilian medical and engineering teams aboard USNS Mercy, one of the US Navy's two 1000 bed floating trauma centers. Along with many others from many nations we were all volunteers on this mission; we were incredibly fortunate to be involved in this experience, but even now---seven years later---many of us still relive the events we were part of during the three months we spent treating some of the poorest people in the world. For the poor there were the hardest hit: the fishermen, the farmers, the struggling workers living from day to day. They were in the middle of a region where rebel (GAM) and nationalist (TNI) forces routinely fought. They were the fodder in the middle of the fight, just wanting to survive and continue to eke out a living. And now, 250,000 of their family members, their friends, their neighbors, their countrymen were dead or missing. But they just carried on, smiling some each day, seeing the bright side of events. After all, they lived...while we cried. They remained stoic, filled with faith, convinced that only God was interested in their well-being. We cried for them, and dared to try helping God with improving their lot.

That is what this book is about.

Everyone has a story; I will attempt in this treatise to try to tell the story of some of those incredible Indonesian people we were privileged to meet during this event. Initially, most of us thought we were just there to help as much as we could and then go home. It was just not that simple.

My participation in the aftermath of the devastating tsunami in Indonesia is the most defining time of my adult life, I think. Doing a television show called "The Mole II," becoming a physician, making Admiral...all were fun and essential parts of my life, truly, but were only prequels to this much more momentous few months. Becoming married forty-two years ago to Shirley, my wife, is central to all of this, and frankly, none of this would have happened without that marriage. I tend to be an extremist in what I do; Shirley has always kept me centered, and has reminded me over the years many times about what is most important. Without her moderation and encouragement, I would have 'extremed' myself right out of my various careers, I think. She also was the reason I got involved with the tsunami relief.

16

On the first of January, 2005, I got an email from the senior 4 star Admiral in the Pacific theater. He was an old friend whom I had not seen in many years, but we had served near each other in Tidewater, VA, in the early to mid1990's. I had retired from the Navy in 1997, and he had gone on to become one of the outstanding leaders of the US Navy. His email was simple and to the point. What was I doing these days?

My response was that I was a consultant to various private enterprises, and occasionally to the Department of Defense. In addition, I told him I was an avid hiker, having just completed the 2174 mile Appalachian Trail the preceding October. His responding email just said that he was in charge of the US response to the tsunami in the Indian Ocean, and he wanted to know if I was available if he needed me. Are you kidding me? Would I help any way I could? Geez, who in the world would pass up such a marvelous opportunity; of course I was available!

Four days later came the call I noted at the beginning of this book.

As I said before, Shirley understands me, and understands that I need to love something to really appreciate it. I loved the Navy, but active duty was long since past. It startled me a little to realize, however, that I had been so transparent about my on-going work projects. She was right; were it not for the money, I would never have thought about any of the jobs for another instant. Most just didn't mean much to me. Being in the Navy wasn't just…a way of life. It *was* life. I loved it, loved the people I worked with (even the ones I didn't like!), and loved the concept of serving the country. I had not found anything that really inspired me since retiring from the Navy. With the exception, of course, of hiking the Appalachian Trail and doing that one TV show. And, those were not a way of life, just goals and fun things to do.

So, I went home, packed my bags, kissed Shirley, and headed off to Hawaii to meet with the Navy folks there. And, true to what Shirley had told them, the money was absolutely not a driving force, and even was somewhat irritating to talk about. I wanted to do this.

I did wind up getting paid, but did not contribute any to the discussion as to how much I would receive. The accounting folks finally threw their hands up and told me what they were going to pay. I said fine, and that was that.

I arrived in Hawaii and was briefed by the Navy medical folks there. USNS Mercy was en route, having passed Hawaii a day before I arrived. The medical folks briefed me on what they knew, which was minimal. By that time it was clear that our activities were going to be confined to the worst hit of the areas in the Indian Ocean, Sumatra, Indonesia. Thailand was doing an excellent job cleaning up its own problems, as was India. Sri Lanka had also been hard hit (31,000 dead), but for political reasons did not want US military involvement there. Indonesia, however, with from 150,000 to 240,000 dead and missing, needed all the help they could get.

USNS Mercy was en route with a skeleton crew of Navy medical personnel, and the promise of about 250 outstanding civilian doctors, nurses, and social workers from around the nation joining them in Singapore. (Strictly speaking, USNS ships are not actually owned by the Navy. They are part of the Merchant Marine Fleet in support of naval activities.) The Chief of Naval Operations had asked Project Hope, a world-wide NGO (non-governmental organization), if they would be interested in putting volunteers aboard Mercy to work, rather than having to get by in primitive conditions in tents ashore. Inasmuch as Mercy is one of two Navy hospital ships, each with 1000 beds and designed as major trauma centers with 12 operating rooms, full diagnostic facilities including CT scanner, and a 6000 unit blood bank capability, the CEO of Project Hope told the CNO that he thought a cooperative venture was a great idea. As it turns out, it was indeed.

All this was fine and dandy, but as I sat receiving briefs and getting the bigger picture, my immediate question was straight forward. What was I supposed to do? Well, in fact none of us were quite sure initially. While I had been on active duty I had taken on a number of troubled organizations and managed with a good team to make them far better ones. I had been the Commanding Officer of the Naval Hospital in Charleston, SC, when Hurricane Hugo hit, and my staff had done an outstanding job following that disaster, which had been well publicized in the Navy. For some reason, both as a Commanding Officer of various commands, and as an Admiral, I had been placed time and again in situations requiring…innovation, I suppose, to recover from. Either someone was trying to send me a message I was too dumb to get or I was just a good scrambler and could salvage…with lots of help…good things out of bad. Regardless, it seemed that here I was in the same situation again. But, as many good people know, where there is a challenge there is opportunity! Admiral Fargo was giving me a most wonderful opportunity!

- - - - - - - -

I would like to note here that I had two secrets of success in the above noted endeavors. First, growing up on a failing farm in Oklahoma with parents who were determined to make it, and determined that their children would make it, might possibly have bequeathed me with a moderate ability to work through tough times (or not). However, when you grow up in a situation that has no excesses…and frequently not enough…of anything, you had best quickly develop an instinct for what works and what doesn't work. There is just not enough flexibility to tolerate many missteps. Perhaps that is one definition of common sense. And, second, I surrounded myself with the best folks I could find and dedicated myself to getting them the tools to do their jobs in the best way they knew how. They seemed to always know that, and almost always exceeded their expectations…though matching the expectations I had of them consistently. When you have people…most of whom are smarter than you…busting their tails to get a job done, and being proud of their efforts, you are going to succeed.

Every time. That was my real secret.

The four star Admiral in charge of the Navy in the Pacific, Admiral Doran, told me that while the President had directed that Mercy respond to the disaster, and all levels of the chain of command were in agreement (Seldom do we disagree with the ultimate Commander-in-Chief!), there was a real concern that Mercy would arrive off the coast of Indonesia and have nothing to do. Whether it would be politics, or a lack of patients, or political pressures from home to bring the ship back immediately (and there were those in the Department of Defense who fought sending the ship over at all, and subsequently fought to limit our effectiveness), if the ship arrived and just...sat there, we would look awfully dumb. So after much discussion, he finally told me to pick an advance team comprised of the expertise I felt I needed, then go to Indonesia and make sure we got to go to work and see patients as soon as the ship arrived.

As I departed his office, he told me, "Bill, I realize that you don't fit anywhere in the chain of command. However, you represent me, and here's my direction: You're in charge of the success of this mission. Make it happen, and let me know if there is any way I can help you toward success."

Little did he know that I would call on him a number of times to correct directives that just didn't meet my definition of common sense. He never failed me.

I picked six people to go with me and help in my efforts. All were active duty except one, Dr. Anne Peterson, a veteran NGO and USAID public health physician. In fact when I called her she was sitting in a Presidential appointee job with USAID. Not knowing her, I was dubious about picking a political person such as Dr. Peterson, but she soon proved to be invaluable in getting us into the doors of the NGO's and UN Agencies we needed to work with. The others, clinicians and administrators from the Navy Department of Medicine, were equally valuable in their areas of expertise, and once I had assessed them, I knew that our part of this endeavor, at least, was going to be okay. I had again picked a team that was better than

20

I was in almost every area; all I had to do was keep folks above them off their backs, and we couldn't fail. And, we didn't.

The details of what we did for the next two weeks are unimportant for this book. We made the rounds of government offices in Jakarta, went to US headquarters in Pattaya Beach, Thailand, consulted with all levels of Sumatran authorities, met with UN agencies and many NGO's…and were met with skepticism and hostility at many levels. However, we persisted in presenting Mercy's potential to all parties. Probably the key decision we made early on was to consistently tell all concerned parties that we understood that we were coming in well after the tsunami, and were there solely to augment their efforts. We were not going to initiate anything new, nor attempt to reinvent a wheel they had rolling fine, nor would we attempt to take over the jobs of any one there. We were willing to fall in behind them, provide them with specialized hospitalization for their patients, manpower for their efforts, diagnostic capabilities far beyond their local capabilities—but only if they wanted them---and specialized medical repair technicians and engineers to repair their equipment if it needed repairs. Of course, after a month in the field, everything they had was broken. It didn't take long before they started looking forward to the arrival of the ship. And, once Mercy arrived, we did exactly as advertised. We helped them in any way possible, and never tried to move anyone aside to place ourselves at center stage. (And, frankly, let's face it. When you are in a huge white ship with red crosses on it, with helicopters flying to and fro continuously, and have capabilities far beyond what anyone else has, you don't need to move anyone out of their comfort zone to be noticed!)

My "situation report" filed with Admiral Doran's staff about this time reveals our activities and concerns at that early point in our relief efforts.

Subject: Sitrep 3 Feb Banda Aceh

("Situational Report" to go to higher ups in the military chain of command) (Usually dry and filled with numbers, and certainly no human interest stories!)

My team is currently aboard Mercy, having transferred over from USS Essex *(an amphibious assault ship)* today. I expect Lincoln is long gone, headed toward Singapore and home. At the moment we are en route around the horn of Sumatra to take up station near Essex, making helo lift tomorrow much quicker and easier.

The last couple of days have been occupied by multiple briefs to and from the senior line commanders in the area to and from the staff aboard Mercy. These gentlemen have the best interests of the mission at heart, clearly, and desire to make sure personnel aboard Mercy have the format down so that all information is considered each day for the next day's mission, and transmitted via an evening VTC (video teleconference). Tonight's first VTC went extremely well, but only after lots of teeth gnashing as the crew here learned a new way of organizing their thoughts! The senior line Marine General, however, was quite complementary of their efforts.

The US Ambassador to Indonesia came aboard today after festivities seeing Lincoln off, and was given an excellent tour of this afloat hospital facility by the hospital CO. Following the tour, the Ambassador addressed all the members of the medical staff, and then held a press conference with visiting press.

We continue to find more patients in our forays ashore. On our last visit to Banda Aceh, 4 more patients were identified who needed our specialized care, making a total of 10 referrals so far. All are quite complex, several direct injuries from the tsunami, the others resulting from being unable to be evaluated by the largely destroyed University Hospital in Banda Aceh.

Hoping for a decision by the GOI (government of Indonesia) to approve the CONOPS (Concept of Operations) soon, we are sending two teams to Banda Aceh tomorrow. One will be clinicians going in to establish more relationships at University Hospital, and to evaluate the patients being referred to Mercy from there. The other is composed of mental health professionals who will start working with professionals from the Psychiatric Hospital (mostly destroyed in the tsunami) associated with the University Hospital. We are also including an epidemiologist on that team. Dr. Peterson will be discussing further cooperative efforts with WHO and UNICEF, both of whom have expressed a strong desire to work with us. They have already screened a great number of sites and should be a significant factor in us becoming much more efficient in our out-reach efforts.

A third helo will fly about 100 miles south, on a low level recon flight to look at the coast. Several members of the staff will be on that helo.

We are hoping to go to work by Saturday. (Actually, a lot of work has occurred already, but by Saturday we hope to be doing what we came for: seeing patients.)

Bill McDaniel

In my last statement I was falsely optimistic; it just seemed to me that it should be common sensical to start doing immediately what we were sent here and charged with doing: seeing patients.

Unfortunately, nothing is that simple!

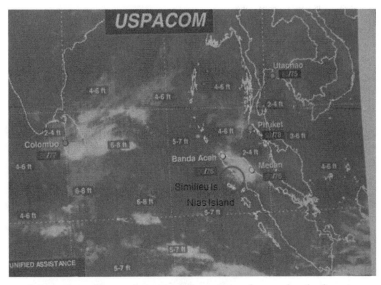

Map showing epicenter of earthquake and relation to
Banda Aceh

Chapter 2

I WOULD LIKE to go over some conditions in Banda Aceh, Indonesia, when I arrived on about 22 January 2005.

The small airport looked sort of like O'Hare airport in Chicago on a busy day. Planes from all over the world landing and taking off, tents everywhere, materials stacked up around the airport in profusion...and apparent confusion, forklifts running back and forth moving gear. It was impressive, and the most impressive aspect of it was that the flags of multiple countries were flying everywhere, all seeming to help each other without regard to country of origin. In the Australian tent hospital on the edge of the field I met medical folks from many countries, all going full blast. I was with an army officer from the US Embassy in Jakarta, assigned to help my team smooth the way for the arrival and acceptance of the hospital ship USNS Mercy.

I had flown from Singapore to the aircraft carrier USS Abraham Lincoln with Dr. Anne Peterson the day before. Landing aboard an aircraft carrier in an "arrested landing" as many have seen on TV is always exciting, and I think that first landing was enough to make the entire trip worthwhile to Anne. (Although she was a trifle disappointed. "Is that all?" I explained to her that for the landing to get more exciting meant that there was a problem, and that kind of excitement we didn't need!) Rear Admiral Doug Crowder and his crew made us very welcome; in fact, they were eager for Mercy to arrive so they could get on with their cruise. They had been at sea for many months, and had been en route to their home port in Washington State when they had been diverted to help with tsunami relief in early January. They had done phenomenal work, delivering over 6,000,000 pounds of food and water to stricken areas, and taking World Health Organization personnel aboard and flying them over Sumatra each day as they mapped and catalogued the incredible damage to about one hundred and twenty-five miles of coast line. (I was told that along the coast highway 97 bridges had been destroyed.) The helo crews from Lincoln and the Marine Amphibious Assault Group and USS Essex had been working at max capacity for three weeks at that point, and were ready for relief.

Anne and I had received extensive briefings the day we arrived, and Admiral Crowder, in accordance with Navy custom, had kept his huge warship stationed about 25 miles out at sea during their maneuvers. While our military customarily responds to disasters all over the world many times a year, we try to do so unobtrusively, and depart as soon as other relief organizations and assets show up with the capability of assuming the relief effort. We seldom get much publicity about our work, and consequently many folks at home and in the affected country are only vaguely aware of our presence initially, if they have any awareness at all. While I suppose this makes sense in many ways, I do feel that we miss a tremendous opportunity for positive publicity in these instances in almost all cases.

This actually wasn't the case in Indonesia, though not of our doing. Both of the major newspapers in Singapore and in Jakarta wrote many stories about the outpouring of assistance from around the world, but their reporters could not help but note near the end of each story that by far the biggest assistance was coming from the US, in the forms of the impressive array of warships and helicopters flying around the country. They reported at length on the capabilities of the Lincoln, and were amazed that the ship could generate 1,000,000 gallons of fresh water daily, which was then distributed around Sumatra in five gallon plastic containers. Lincoln was able to keep almost all the isolated affected areas plentifully supplied with good water, contributing greatly to the prevention of the widely predicted multiple disease epidemics that many felt were inevitable. They just didn't happen. And, while UNICEF and other organizations did incredible work in giving mass immunizations to almost 1,000,000 people over the two months there, it was still the ready availability of fresh uncontaminated water that might be the primary reason those epidemics were nipped before they started.

So, in this case, the US efforts were actually well known, and well appreciated.

Some interesting facts about Indonesia should be pointed out. I expect most everyone is aware that there has been a rebel separatist movement in Sumatra for about thirty years, with the goal of separating that island from the rest of Indonesia as a separate nation. (Cynics might note that the fact that Sumatra has the biggest deposits of oil and natural gas in that part of the world could be a part of the reason Jakarta did not view this separatist movement with favor.) Indonesia is the most populous Moslem nation in the world, and the entire country is very, very conservative. Military-to-military relations between the US and Indonesia used to be very constructive, but were suspended many years before this. (In fact, the only military presence tolerated was our NAMRU-2 Naval Medical research unit in Jakarta, which was highly regarded by the host country. Many of the Ministers of Health in the last 40 years have been graduates of a one year internship there, and proudly display those certificates in the ministry offices.)

Overall, the USA was not overly popular in Indonesia; there was only about a 25% approval rating toward America there. On the other hand, Bin Laden was highly revered. In no place were these perceptions more pronounced than in Sumatra. Most of the average citizens thought of America only as the "great Satan," inasmuch as that is all they had heard about us. For weeks, however, they had seen the gray helicopters with USA markings delivering food, water, and medical teams to the most severely disadvantaged among them, so a different attitude might be forthcoming from this. Or not.

There are over 17,000 islands compromising Indonesia, about 200,000,000 people, and more languages and dialects than one could count...certainly over 300. And, as everyone knows, Indonesia historically has been subject to the most severe of natural disasters, from the Krakatoa explosion on August 6, 1883, to hurricanes, floods, tsunamis, and earthquake after earthquake. When an overloaded ferry capsizes in the world, odds are good that it is Indonesian.

This earthquake was no exception; indeed, it seemed to follow the natural rules that Indonesia lives under. At about 6:58 (or 7:58 in Banda Aceh) on Sunday morning, 26 December 2004, an earthquake measuring about 9.3 shook that part of the world; in fact, it shook the entire world! (This was the second strongest earthquake ever recorded in the world, exceeded only by a 9.5 earthquake in Chile in 1960. Experts have some disagreement as to the exact strength of the Indian Ocean earthquake; estimates range from 9.0 to 9.3.) With an epicenter just off Simeulue Island, about 135 miles south of Banda Aceh, conditions were perfect for the development of the most feared aftermath of an sub-oceanic earthquake, a tsunami. (Of interest, however, is that the tsunami did not adversely affect Simeulue Island; instead the island rose about 5 meters in height and became several kilometers longer!) A 1200 (or 1600, depending on the source) kilometer long tectonic shelf which had been slowly trying to glide up over another tectonic plate suddenly gave way, slipping about 15 meters in an instant with an upward surge. Water doesn't compress well; in fact, it doesn't. Compress, that is. If there is a sudden movement of the land under the water, the water moves up as well...rapidly. Within moments a 150 foot high wave was generated at the epicenter, with an initial estimated speed of about 500 miles per hour as it moved out northward, spreading both to the east and to the west. Of course, as the water dragged across the ocean bottom, friction slowed it considerably, but it was to impact the shores of Sumatra at speeds approaching 80 mph, and with a height of 60+ feet. (Unofficial reports in Banda Aceh stated that the waves that hit there were as high as 65 feet. There is evidence that the wave towered to as much as 100 feet high in some spots in Sumatra.) This is somewhat like being hit by a massive freight train traveling at that speed...only much worse. The hilly, forested shorelines of 125 miles of Sumatra were totally denuded of trees up to as high as 150 feet in some places, and any buildings encountered simply...vanished. Any rubble was either piled up several miles inland (in the case of Banda Aceh) when the wave finally subsided, or was sucked back out to sea, along with 10's of thousands of the people living along that shoreline. And we always discuss only the tsunami, forgetting the incredible power of the earthquake that preceded it, which itself must have caused unthinkable damage and deaths. Those were all obscured forever, however, by the massive onslaught of water we call a tsunami.

The death toll in Indonesia will never be known with certainty. Government estimates are about 167,000 people killed (bodies recovered) and as many as 127,000 just missing, either resting at sea or perhaps displaced to another part of Indonesia. Truly, trying to get exact figures for the speed and height of the waves, and for the number of folks killed is impossible. Some figures are solid, but there are just too many unknowns to result in exact figures. (As noted, even the experts cannot agree on the exact strength of the initiating earthquake!)

I mentioned earlier that the entire world was affected. There was not a land mass in the world that did not move up and down at least a centimeter as a consequence of this massive earthquake. Worldwide, there is an earthquake somewhere about every 4 minutes. This one earthquake, however, unleashed more power that all the earthquakes in the world together over the 5 years preceding this! The world truly did ring like a bell struck by a very big hammer.

As I worked this mission, I would send an occasional update to email acquaintances back in the states. I will include these in appropriate places as I proceed.

6 Feb 2005 Off Banda Aceh

It's been a few days since I first wrote all of you and told you I was becoming involved with this disaster relief mission. I will not bore you with the endless politics of attempting to do something like this. Honestly, had I known I would have had to sit through so many meetings and give the same explanations to so many people, I might have gone back to the Appalachian Trail. However, we finally got all the visits made that had to be made to start our real work here in Sumatra. It was worth it.

I'll start at the end of our first day of receiving patients. Just as our team was leaving Abidin Hospital on our first visit, an 11 year old boy came in with a ruptured appendix; he was severely septic. The two operating rooms there were full, and our folks were asked if we could take him for surgery. Not a problem, as you might imagine! He and his father were brought to USNS Mercy; he was obviously severely ill. The father was quite upset, and the interpreters told us that his wife and all other children had been lost in the tsunami. This was the only child left; he was soon taken to surgery, and the father went to the chapel to pray. His prayers worked. A Navy surgeon and a Project Hope surgeon operated upon his son successfully, removing a perforated appendix. The child is doing fine now.

30

Today we admitted a 12 year old boy, Iqbal, whose entire family was killed in the tsunami; he clung to a piece of driftwood for a day following the tsunami, and was found about 2 kilometers from the shore by some fishermen. He has been ill since, and today suffered a respiratory arrest at University Hospital. We happened to have 30 or so of our folks working there helping to get the facility functional, and one of our helos was on the pad with rotors turning. The child was rushed to Mercy, where he was given intensive treatment by infectious disease and pulmonary doctors. He is on a respirator. He has a chance, but is severely malnourished and has a white count of 85,000 (normal is about 5000).

We have several other patients here, with several surgeries today and multiple surgeries planned for tomorrow. Morale is high on Mercy; the harder the folks work, the happier they seem to be. (By that criterion, I should be most happy by this point.) I haven't worked hours this long in many years. And, everyone else is working harder.

I mentioned University (Abidin) Hospital, where we are concentrating most of our efforts. The tsunami came through and filled all the rooms of this huge one story teaching hospital with 8 feet of mud and water. All the staff and patients in the facility died. Every one. That was 400 patients and about half the 900 staff, and since then only about 200 staff have reappeared. No one knows where the rest are. The director, Dr. Rus, is an amazing man. He lost his entire family and home, yet was back at the hospital directing clean-up efforts the next day. He has stayed at it since then; maybe this is his therapy for such a loss. He is remarkable; I enjoy talking with him. The Australians, Germans, Belgians, New Zealanders, and Russians have all done a tremendous job in helping rehabilitate his facility.

Many feet of mud...and many bodies...have been removed. Wards are back in use. We are now at 150 beds, down from the original 450, but better than no beds at all. All equipment has been destroyed. A (formerly) new CT scanner is now a coffee table. Three dialysis units gone. Everything was buried under many feet of dark, smelly, foul, mud. As I noted, we are concentrating our efforts here, where we think we will have a lasting effect for years to come. Project Hope doctors work with us, and they are going to seek sources of donations and partnering. I have not seen a more deserving facility. Nor a more deserving director.

I find it almost impossible to describe the scene within 2-4 miles of the beach. You all have seen pictures, but the pictures are not....big enough. The catastrophe is almost unimaginable. You drive out to where the shoreline is now and look around. It looks like something from a movie about the end of the world. I have pictures, lots of pictures.

What I can't capture on film is the smell. Thousands and thousands of bodies have been removed, but many more remain. Buildings that collapsed in the earthquake have not been touched...nor those in them. No one is out there. They are all dead. Few people look.

Yet, life only a few miles away goes on at a frantic pace. The people are delightful, nice, open, and apparently happy to see us. No anti-American spirit evident here. Traffic is impossible. Every driver seems to think he is on a qualifying run for a Grand Prix event, especially the daredevils on mopeds. Maybe they have seen so much death and destruction that they feel...like nothing can touch them. Or, maybe they just get on with life. There is little alternative, after all.

By the way, I got my hair cut before Mercy arrived by a twenty-six year old Aceh barber. He spoke perfect English, oddly enough. This little known part of Indonesia teaches English in its schools. Amazing. And incidentally, he has a non-union of a femur fracture. He deserves to be well, so we try to remedy that problem. Shoot, you've got to take care of your barber!

I wish you could all be part of this. Maybe, if I'm any good at all, I can allow you that wish with these notes.

Bill McDaniel

Major General Harold Timbo, Master of the Mercy Nate
Smith, and Rear Admiral Bill McDaniel

Chapter 3

Y OU KNOW, I have delayed trying to write this book because I got…we all got…so emotionally involved in this effort. In the plight of the Indonesian people. In our own very shaky mortality. In everything. At this moment, having reviewed my photos in attempting to even remotely explain what we did, what we felt there, I am overwhelmed by emotion. And this is years later. Several months ago some friends asked me to read some of the emails aloud that I had written and sent out; you will eventually see most of them here. I started reading, and within minutes put the papers down and apologized; I could not read them aloud. I couldn't see through the tears.

The fits and starts of getting such an effort under way as we were doing were frustrating. The initial resistance was from the people from all nations ashore, angry because we were so late, then sure we were going to try to come in and "suck up all the glory."

There was tragedy enough to go around. Then, their acceptance as we steadfastly continued to offer our tremendous capabilities to them, but only if they needed them. Our commitment was to fall in behind them and contribute what we could to the effort. Fairly quickly they came to understand this, though there were exceptions, as there always are.

Doctors without Borders, who do a wonderful job worldwide. They needed refrigerators to store vaccines in, and there were no spares available ashore. However, aboard our 1000 bed trauma center we had huge walk-in freezers which could have handled anything. I offered these up to a representative of Doctors without Borders one day, and she apologetically told me that they would not work with any military...and especially from the US. Does this make sense? Not to me. When we have a crisis situation like this, perhaps Doctors without Borders would be better served to "get over it."

My team lived aboard USS Abraham Lincoln for the first two weeks or so, before transitioning to another of the amphibious ships, USS Essex for a day or two, then to USNS Mercy when she arrived. We were treated royally by the staffs of both ships, who had been working unending hours in the month they had been off the coast of Sumatra. They were eager to hand off this effort to us so they could get on with their cruise...a return home after 8 months in the Gulf.

For some reason the Marine amphibious group was assigned to oversee our small four ship armada for the first eight days we were there. I am not sure why; probably because they had been there since early January and were to provide an overlap and impart some badly needed local knowledge to us that we needed to get our jobs done. That made sense, so far as it went.

However, keep in mind that my advance team had been ashore since about 22 January, and by the time Mercy arrived on 3 February the hospitals ashore realized that the only chance of keeping a number of their patients alive was for us to take them off their hands immediately. We had the specialists, the diagnostic and treatment equipment, and certainly room enough. So, those medical personnel ashore were eagerly awaiting the arrival of helicopters on 4 February to start ferrying critically ill patients seaward.

That didn't happen.

The Marines came aboard, and the very competent Marine General immediately called the senior medical staff together and explained that there was a right way to do our mission, and his staff was going to teach that way to us. They did that, and rightly so. However, as dedicated as they may have been to helping us do our job, our only real task ultimately consisted of seeing patients, which we were restricted from doing for several days. Why? I'm not sure. I think they were eagerly looking forward to getting home, and they would be allowed to head that way after overseeing us for 8 days. They had been working hard for a month, and their helicopter crews and machines alike were well used and in need of rest.

Fine and dandy. But, we had not been working. All of the medical staff had been riding the ship and taking part in endless exercises, which are all part of our required and needed training, but lead you to want to get to the real thing as quickly as possible. Plus, I had been going ashore daily for almost 2 weeks along with several clinicians planning which patients we needed to evacuate first in order to save as many as possible. We were ready to see patients…regardless of the paperwork.

What we got was education. Repeatedly. And, for four straight mornings, excuses that "our" helicopters were not in a ready status yet. We did have some outstanding Marines working with us, trying hard to get us functioning; I think it was just inertia and fatigue that caused the others to delay actual movement of staff and patients. What they clearly did not recognize was that their delaying tactics, no matter how valid their reasoning, were allowing patients to die ashore. On the 3rd evening after Mercy's arrival, one of the sharper ship's docs who had been going ashore with me came over.

"Admiral, I'm embarrassed; I just don't want to go to shore again until we are truly ready to bring patients aboard. I just can't bear to have them look out at us and ask why we aren't honoring our promises."

I agreed.

On the fourth morning I was informed that, once again, our helicopters were not ready. Now, I had no official place in the chain of command in this effort. But, I did have a few ways that I might be able to push things.

The foremost factor working for me was having ADM Doran tell me I was in charge of the "success" of the mission. Make it happen and he would back me. In the military when the senior ranking officer in the Pacific tells you he has your back, it does help matters a tad. And, even though I was retired, I was still the senior officer in the area. Retired or not, we all know who is around. I had served with the Marines in Viet Nam and had tremendous respect for them. However, as any Marine will tell you, it helps to be able to speak their language. My Marine pilots in Viet Nam had taught me 'Marine' talk well!

So, I approached the senior Marine assigned to us, an 0-6, who was all smiles. He knew who I was, though we had never spoken. As noted before, I was not part of the official chain of command, and did not sit in on most meetings.

"COL, where are our helos?"

"Doc, I'm sorry, but we're trying to keep this realistic; the two helos assigned to you are undergoing some mechanical things. We'll get there; relax!"

"COL, let me explain something to you."

He started to speak. "COL, don't say anything. This is a monologue, not a dialogue."

"Do you understand what happens every day you pull this crap?"

"People die. Every single day. People that we have evaluated the day before and have solemnly sworn to take aboard this very elegant trauma center and try to save. COL, I don't care if your folks are tired. That's not my problem. My problem is that you are not giving us the support we have to have to do this job. We've done all the paper work; it's long past time that we start saving lives. So, here's what I suggest you do. Call one of your working helos over from your ship and get off Mercy. Don't come back until you are ready to be part of the solution, and not part of the problem."

I must admit to using somewhat saltier language than represented here. I love the Marines and think they are the greatest fighting force we have; so effective communication is essential when dealing with them.

The COL had turned a little white during my monologue. I gave him no time to attempt an answer, but turned and walked away. He called in a helo and left the ship.

Meanwhile, I looked up the ship's Master, a Naval Academy graduate of 1974, a wonderful man with great common sense, then in the Military Sealift Command, and a civilian. We discussed the situation as I attempted to calm down, but I was really, really pissed. We looked up the poor Air Operations Officer, a LCDR from the amphibious group, and talked with him. He was near tears when we left.

The Master and I sat in his office and had coffee; he made great coffee, and I love coffee at any time! I excused myself and went across the hall to my room.

I thought about it a moment, then composed an email to the Deputy Cinc (Commander in Chief Pacific) (number two Admiral in the chain of command) in Hawaii. I asked him not to *necessarily* act on my email; I was just using him to express my frustration. However, I did point out to him that I had fulfilled my part of the job; I had found patients and had acquired the acceptance from the international community for our presence. The problem we were running into went directly back to the promise that had been made to me; if I would find the patients, we would receive the support needed to care for them. I strongly suggested that if we could not get immediate helo support we should withdraw Mercy over the horizon so it would not be visible from shore. No sense in courting further embarrassment.

The DCinc was a smart man. He got the message loud and clear, and not only got it, was probably as irritated as I was. Early the next morning we had more helicopter support than we could ever totally use, and got to start our real work in Banda Aceh. Saving lives and making a difference.

Below is a report I sent to senior officials shortly before this.

Sitrep 5 Feb Banda Aceh

Well, things are looking up in Banda Aceh. After a day of some turmoil with the CONOPS (plan of operations) approval process, most of the staff had become resigned to the likelihood that we would be unable to see patients until early in the week. Morale on board is poor. However, with the restriction to our activities being that we could not engage in patient care, there were still lots of possible ways we could assist the people of Banda Aceh. We sent two helos in today, with a total of 20 people. Unfortunately, due to diversions of one of the helos and mechanical problems with the others, several meetings were missed. However, we did accomplish quite a lot. We have been assured that all attempts will be made to keep the helos up and running, and on time.

Some general problems were identified; as usual, the biggest problem was reliable communications. It is frequently impossible to call from the ship to the shore, and vice versa. Just the vagaries of this part of the world. We also had problems with our two Iridium phones. It is mandatory that we greatly improve our comms capabilities, and this is being worked aggressively. I expect things to improve tomorrow. Having adequate comms capabilities is both a logistics and a safety issue. We hope to soon send every team out with an Iridium phone. In addition, we are still struggling with manifest changes (which personnel to send in), but that is also a learning evolution, and I expect will smooth out quickly.

1. The nursing team leader met with the Indonesian nurses at the University hospital (Abidin Hospital), using one of our translators for communications. (The translators were invaluable in our overall effort.) They established a list of equipment and supplies needed in the emergency room. There is a request for 6-10

nurses to help supplement the current staff during the day shift. We will work toward meeting that need immediately.

2. Medical repair technicians checked over a non-operative mobile X-ray unit, and had it fixed and working properly after a short while.

-They identified a number of repairs needed in the University Hospital, and will travel in daily working on them, greatly improving the basic operating systems of the hospital.

-All the hospitals in Banda Aceh have a shortage of oxygen, and we brought 4 oxygen tanks here from the Indonesians, Germans, and Australians. Our engineers have modified the valves so we can fill them and they can be used back in their facilities. There is a surplus of bottles; we will fill 30-40, which will suffice for a couple of weeks at a time.

-One of the big items is a cold chain room for handling and storing vaccines. The Australians had fixed the refrigerator at Abadin Hospital, and our techs will work on the transport boxes tomorrow.

-They examined the anesthesia machines, finding them operative, but missing many of the accessory items. They are low on consumables, many of which we can replace.

3. Two engineers from Mercy went in and checked out their oxygen bottles, medical vacuum pumps, and air compressors. They reported that the damage done by the mud--up to 8 feet deep--was immense, but they are returning tomorrow with an electrician, a plumber, and another technician to work on this equipment. Some equipment will be brought back to the ship for more definitive repair.

-The transformer room is full of mud, and we are working with the Germans trying to fix it. There is a need for calcium hypochlorite for the water reservoir, which we can supply.

4. A pharmacist and a pharmacy tech went in to look at their pharmacy. The original one had been totally destroyed, and both pharmacists died in the tsunami. There are 4 women working there attempting to clean up a storeroom, but they have no pharmacy

training. The first thing that is needed for the storeroom conversion is construction of shelves. Project Hope will contribute the money needed for construction, and the Australians will hire some local contractors they use to come in and build all new shelving in the pharmacy. Our pharmacy personnel will assist in the design, and will categorize and stock the pharmacy once that is done. They will go back in tomorrow to hire the contractor.

5. Our Out-Reach team got an extremely late start due to helo problems, missing two meetings. They also had comms problems during the day. They went to UNICEF and worked with the CDC (Center for Disease Control) folks who are working there, and identified several items needing attention.

-There appears to be a dengue outbreak south of Banda, and the local folks are investigating. When the time comes, our folks may travel to Simeuleu Island with them to work this issue.

-The IDP (internal displaced persons) camps need risk and threat assessments for water and diseases, and they will work with the Australians who have been covering the area on this issue.

6. Mental health: The head of UNICEF (Claudia Hudspeth) here met with our mental health team for 2 hours going over problems that need addressing. She is a phenomenally well organized person, and a pleasure to work with.

-One of the areas they will be addressing is the 15,000 displaced children in the area. There are also 20 child care centers in the area, whose function is to try to return those children to their families, if they still exist.

-Another area requiring mental health outreach is the schools, where it is estimated that 50% of the students are dead or missing. They will initiate programs for the traumatized teachers and children. They will facilitate social support for the teachers, and will assist the Indonesian NGO's with current concepts. Family support will also be initiated and re-established from the ground up.

-A troubling area is child sexual exploitation. It is estimated that 700 children have been abducted from this area since the tsunami. They are trying to come up with programs to assist in this area.

-The NGO's are requesting crisis and grief counseling for themselves, which we will begin this week.

7. Dental needs are paramount in this area. The university has 10 dental chairs, and one provider. We will initiate assistance using their chairs. Our dental tech repaired their air compressor today.

8. Our recon and future ops team attended the UN representative meeting and the civil-military meeting. They feel that transportation and logistics support are connecting well, but feel again that we need a permanent detachment ashore to coordinate with these folks, and attend the coordination meetings we cannot get to now. This has been a disapproved item in the past, but we need to revisit it.

Tomorrow looks to be a busy day. We have a senior military official coming for a visit. We also have two waves of visitors to the ship; these will be the leaders of all the big NGO's and UN agencies in town, as well as USAID, the leaders of the hospitals and the German hospital ship, representatives of the Ministry of Health, and representatives of TNI (Indonesian military). Pak Budi, the head of the FEMA equivalent, could not come tomorrow, but may come on Monday. We will host these individuals in 2 groups, for 2 hours each group.

In addition, we are sending 3 teams to Banda Aceh.

1. The hospital team consists of dentists, dental techs, optometrists and techs, 3 Project Hope nurses, communications technicians, a supply officer, and 2 navy nurses.

2. Out-reach personnel will go in to continue to coordinate their efforts with their counterparts at UNICEF.

3. Communications folks are going to aggressively work the comms problems. In addition, the engineers and bio medical technicians are returning to continue their efforts to repair the damaged equipment in the University hospital.

We will (hopefully) start moving patients to the ship on Monday.

The Commanding Officer of the Mercy Hospital met with the Vice President of Indonesia at the University hospital, and had a very cordial discussion with him. The CO again expressed our sadness at what had happened here. He reported that the VP was extremely cordial, and may wish to visit Mercy at a later date.

Finally, as is known by all addressees, we got word early in the afternoon that the GOI (Government of Indonesia) had approved our CONOPS (Concept of Operations), resulting in many very happy faces in personnel aboard Mercy. Many thanks to all who made this possible.

W. J. McDaniel
As I have noted, lots of moving parts to this operation.

I casually passed over our efforts to repair medical equipment ashore above. Before Mercy arrived I had visited the International Red Cross Hospital (a many-tented affair) and toured it with the Commanding Officer, a Norwegian COL. He had explained to me that his instructions were to work independently of the US military, and USNS Mercy. Politics, you know. Political correctness (a four letter word if I have ever heard one). So, he would be unable to cooperate with us actively. I acknowledged his explanation, and then asked how his equipment was holding out in this hot, humid climate? He noted that none of his X-ray units were functional…and they were the most advanced diagnostic equipment he had!

The next day I returned with several of our X-ray techs and medical repair techs. I explained to him that I totally understood his inability to cooperate with us, but wondered if my folks could look at his X-ray equipment? Not knowing how to refuse gratefully he mumbled an acceptance. Within about four hours all his machines were working. I then told him that while appreciating the politics of his position, unofficially we would always be available to help him if he had problems. He had seen the incredible value of working together already, and indicated that we should continue to do so.

I assured him that we could do so, and the ICRC became our most valuable partner in the relief effort.

This was a great example of the problems we face when responding to international crisis situations. Our capabilities are always greater than anyone else has. We can always do an outstanding job...by ourselves. We aren't so good at "playing nicely with others." Not that we are rude; we just by and large ignore them and do our own thing...which, as noted, is superb work. However, if we really want to continue building true international support and cooperative ventures with other responders, we have to learn to communicate better than we ordinarily do. This endeavor was marked by the foresight of two 4 star Admirals in the Pacific who foresaw this possibility and attempted to find a solution.

I would like to say that we have continued this cooperative venture in subsequent disasters. We have not done so. We continue our overwhelming and effective response, but do not reach out very much to the other international players present.

Too much effort?

Not enough payoff?

Not really needed?

Well, those decisions are part of our national strategy and are way above my pay grade. I will say that it really does not take much effort to make the transition to "cooperative partners" vice "those big guys on the block who do not notice us!"

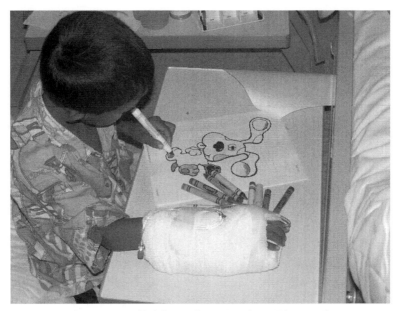

First appendicitis patient, Wahyu Firmanda

Chapter 4

THE MORNING FOLLOWING our new-found influx of helicopters (February seventh) we were working, and working hard. The logistics of such an effort are complex. We did have enough helos assigned to get all of us back and forth, but had to determine who were best utilized ashore, and who could best be utilized aboard ship. (Each flight, for some reason unknown to me, was called a "stick.") Clearly, everyone wanted to go ashore; that was where the action was, and while the damage could be seen from the ship, it was unreal up close. However, that was not to be; the majority of the personnel never got ashore, except when coming and going home. After all, this was a working trip, not a cruise.

At a 6:00 PM meeting every evening, representatives from all departments and from Project Hope would meet and go over the plans for the next day. Helo flights had to be carefully orchestrated, inasmuch as we frequently sent 70 or so folks to various sites ashore in waves (sticks) of twelve at a time, and were to start retrieving patients almost immediately, some of whom would be coming back with medical escorts, and always with a 'healthy' family member. (We screened all family members, and wound up doing a surprising amount of work on the healthy one of the two! Plus, an incredible number of them tested positive for tuberculosis, and we had to then evaluate them to see if they had active disease that needed to be treated. All the while the patient and family member both had to wear isolation masks so as to not spread disease, and if active TB were found, they were then isolated in the negative pressure rooms aboard ship. Not your standard simple admission.) Another decision we consciously made was to not check HIV status on our incoming patients. No one knows what the incidence is in that part of the world, and for many reasons, both political and medical, we did not want to pave the way. So, we just decided to treat every case as if they might be HIV positive, thereby double gloving when doing surgery and taking great care with sharp instruments. I've often thought that we might have missed a great opportunity to determine the prevalence of HIV there, but to what end? Academia only. We couldn't treat them, the Indonesians couldn't treat them, and the political ramifications from raising the issue just had no positive outcomes. So, we avoided it...wisely, I think.

On top of all of this was the need to allow visitors from other nations to see the ship, as well as those from the host nation. Plus reporters and photographers. Most of the volunteer medical personnel from around the world had been living in tents for 6 weeks or so, and had not had a good meal or a hot shower. In addition to getting to see the capabilities of Mercy, they were often found taking their 10th or so hot shower of the day, or sitting in the quietness of the air-conditioned library, reading. The ship became a welcome sanctuary to lots of folks, and that sanctuary was all part of our being accepted and appreciated by the other nations.

Important as all the traffic back and forth to the ship was, we were still in constant motion, sailing up and down 3-5 miles off shore. There were no deep water piers to tie up to, and for security reasons it was elected to not anchor. Plus, there were emergency flights almost daily.

We had just landed our first teams ashore, and coordination efforts were underway to make rounds on patients at Abidin Hospital and the TNI military hospital. (There had been 5 hospitals in Banda Aceh prior to the tsunami; 2 were totally destroyed, and a private hospital about half destroyed. We visited the private facility, but they wanted to remain…very private.)

As an outstanding Navy nurse (CDR Karen McDonald) went into the Abidin Hospital ER to visit and see if they had anyone who needed reviewing, she was approached immediately by the American doctor who was there running the ER. He had been on site since shortly after the tsunami, and had no association with us.

"CDR, we have a little boy here who has a ruptured appendix, is septic, and who will die if we can't get immediate surgery done."

A very ill little boy was lying there, hot with fever, and a father sitting quietly next to him.

The ER physician continued, "This is the only family member besides the father who survived the tsunami. All of his brothers and sisters, and his mother, died that day."

Well, clearly we were going to take this kid, but this sort of added to the urgency.

The nurse ran out the ER, and about 100 yards away noted a US helicopter settling on the landing pad near the hospital. The one star Marine general strode off, eager to see how things were going ashore on this first day of real activity. She ran up to him.

"General, we have a little boy who is dying, right now. We need your helicopter, now, please."

He immediately told her to take it and go, and he would help anyway he could.

We got the little boy on board within minutes, and within an hour he was in surgery. The father looked around this huge facility, somewhat dazed, unable to speak our language and knowing only that his dying son had just disappeared down a hallway. One of the

Bahasa Indonesia translators explained to him what was going on, then led him down to the ward to await the child's return from surgery.

Inasmuch as we were dealing with very devout Moslems, we had established a small prayer room for their use. We drew an arrow on one wall and told them that represented 'East,' which their religion dictates they face in prayer. Now, these were intelligent folks, and we were on a ship constantly underway going in big circles. There was no way that that wall always faced East....unless that room had mystical qualities...that such a religious room *might* have had. Regardless, all the folks who used it resolutely faced that wall, prayed, and seemed to be comforted.

This father stayed there for 2 days, emerging only when he had to. His son come out of surgery, still quite ill, but within 48 hours was up and about. Dad's prayers seemed to have worked!

(A brief note on language. The local language was referred to as "Bahasa." Bahasa just means "language." So, to correctly identify the language spoken, one should refer to "Bahasa Indonesia," or the Indonesian language. For the sake of simplicity for this tome, I will only refer to it as "Bahasa.")

Sitrep 7 Feb Banda Aceh

Again, let me start at the end of the day; after all, the final results are frequently the determination of success. In mid-afternoon there was an emergency medevac from University Hospital to Mercy. A 12 year old boy had been swept away in the tsunami, along with his entire family. He survived by hanging on to a piece of wood for the better part of a day, and was finally rescued about 2 kilometers from shore by some local fishermen. All of his immediate family died. He had inhaled lots of water, and has had problems since that time. His uncle brought him to the University Hospital 10 days ago with severe pneumonia, but in the last day he suddenly began to decompensate. Today, while about 30 of our personnel were working at the hospital, the boy suffered a pulmonary arrest and was immediately intubated by the Australians. They asked us to do an emergency transfer so that our infectious disease and pulmonary specialists might offer him a slim chance to live. We did so. Currently the young man is intubated, on respiratory assistance, and is under intensive care by specialists here. His chances are slim, but if he can be saved, our team will make that happen.

Our appendicitis patient from last night is doing super, and the nurses are spoiling both him and his father. Quite a feat when there is no common language, but they are managing quite nicely.

A patient was admitted with a mandible fracture, and our Navy oral surgeon is in surgery with him as I type this. The Navy orthopedic surgeon and the Project Hope orthopedic surgeon operated upon a patient with a broken tibia and placed a rod in it. That patient is doing well also. We admitted a patient with severe burns and contractures, and soon our surgeons and plastic surgeons will start releasing those contractures. Finally, we admitted a patient with a perforated gastric ulcer to the ICU; I'm surprised we don't see more of these. The Indonesians have an amazingly positive attitude. Family members accompany each patient, and are all quite positive. Our interpreters are kept busy translating, and are doing an excellent job.

1. Nine nurses and corpsmen accompanied UNICEF today and gave over 200 immunizations. (With 1.3 million children to vaccinate, about 70,000 have been done. So, we continue to have work to do in this area.)

2. Our ophthalmologist and an optometrist examined and fitted glasses for 40 patients today, and lined up 5 for cataract surgery for Friday. Both the Navy and the Project Hope ophthalmologists will operate upon the patients, and the numbers are expected to greatly increase over the next several weeks. They are forming an operative team for this effort.

3. At Abidin hospital the pharmacist and his tech inventoried over 91 medications and categorized them today, and will review another 600 or so in the next few days.

4. The engineers and medical techs continued to repair equipment, with all the equipment brought to the ship yesterday being taken back to the hospital and put to use. They validated an ESU (electrical surgical) unit for the operating room. The ER refrigerator was checked over and cleaned, and will be monitored. The pharmacy A/C unit was repaired and is in good working order.

The portable X-ray unit has a bad fuse, and the team is trying to locate a replacement fuse. They overhauled the sewage pump and will reinstall on site. They also obtained a fuse for the main power grid, and obtained replacement parts for four motors in the central air/vacuum distribution facility. They continue to do outstanding work in helping to bring this facility back to full function.

5. My team met for an hour with the Vice Minister of Banda Aceh Provincial Health Office, as well as the Vice Minister of the Ministry of Health from Jakarta. We took great care in presenting to them our proposed plans to work closely with local NGO's in their efforts and locations, and explained our plan of admitting all patients to Mercy through the auspices of Dr. Rus, the Director of the University Hospital. In the end they gave us a green light for our proposals, assuming that we have TNI approval, of course.

-We met with Dr. Rus at the University, and had an excellent discussion. He asked if there were any possibilities of getting some funding for some of his problems, and if there is a possibility of teaming with a University in the states. On Wednesday I am returning to discuss this with two Project Hope physicians who have some ideas on these issues.

-We met at the Monday meeting of all interested NGO and hospital personnel from the entire Banda Aceh area for an hour, and presented to them the capabilities of Mercy. We were again well received.

-We met again for another 2 hours with organizations working to improve University Hospital, and again made a presentation. There are some outstanding efforts being made there, especially by the Australians and Germans.

-In the afternoon we met with Doctors without Borders. It was an amiable meeting, but will be unlikely to produce any results.

6. We are considering holding another open house. Apparently word has spread, and we have been approached by lots of folks who want to come out and see the facility.

7. Procedures have been firmly established on how to handle an Indonesian death on board.

8. Dental saw 12 patients today, resulting in an unknown number of missing teeth.

Tomorrow we again have teams going to the University hospital totaling 39 people. I will accompany a team going to Lamno to examine 4 patients the Pakistani Hospital wants us to take. We will also interview the local NGO's to see if we can aid them any there.

Morale is high, helos are working well, and comms are good.

Bill McDaniel

Part of the very interesting work in doing such a mission as ours is trying to decide which of our legalities to impose on the host nation! For instance, what about "informed consent" when we are going to do surgery? Do we take our very complex outline of every possible complication ever recorded, translate it to Bahasa, then try to make the locals understand it and sign it? All this when they have never seen a legal document or a lawyer in their lives? (Lucky folks.) While working with interpreters who have no comprehension of what the document is or why we are trying to unnecessarily complicate their lives by demanding it of them?

The result was just a short consent form, simply saying that we are going to do our best to help them. This they did understand. The lawyers were a little concerned, however. If this caught on they might have to find another line of work!

The other sticky point was the procedures we would follow in event of a death of an Indonesian on board Mercy. Again, luckily, common sense prevailed and we kept it simple. They were used to death, and had seen lots of it. If we just respected their dignity and desires to die on home soil when possible, we would do fine. We did that, and never had any problems with this.

Prepared to fly...with apprehension

Chapter 5

I SENT MISSIVES out about every 10 days to 2 weeks to email friends around the world, trying to keep them up...somewhat...with our progress. However, I sent daily "sitreps" (situation reports) out to the military chain of command above me. Inasmuch as there were multiple levels of reports going to those same individuals from various commands on and off the ship, I felt no need to make my reports dry and didactic, filled with numbers and statistics. I really felt it was important to allow all those folks to understand fully that this was a *people* endeavor, and statistics, numbers, procedures, and other usual reporting data were the least important of what we were doing. (While strongly suspecting that they were more interested in the numbers and not my stories!) We were treating people, interacting with people, saving people, hopefully making new friends. The people involved, both those

53

treating and those being treated, were the most important aspects of this effort.

I tried to build on each day's sitrep when I wrote the next day's report. I wanted to tell a continuing story of these incredible people we were involved with, and report both the successes and failures; both were important.

As noted earlier, there was some legal consternation initially about what we would have to do if a patient died aboard ship. Lawyers wrung their hands about how we should handle such an event. Well, folks, these people had seen approximately 250,000 of their friends, family, and countrymen die in one fell swoop. They dealt with the continuing war between the rebels (GAM) (Free Aceh Movement) and the army, with them frequently in the middle as fodder for both sides. They understood death, if nothing else. If someone died…they died.

What they were *not* accustomed to was people being deeply concerned about their welfare and their *being*, and about them as individuals. So, day after day we had ill and injured patients and their families with great trepidation being flown aboard Mercy; few had ever seen a helicopter, let alone flown in one. Nor a ship the size of Mercy. Nor a ship full of Americans from all heritages, but clearly no one like them. Indeed, foreigners from a country most of them had heard referred to only as "The Great Satan." They came aboard scared and confused, hoping that someone might be able to address their problems.

What did they get? Deeply concerned medical, shipboard, and engineering folks all hoping to be able to help them somehow. They got incredibly caring and sympathetic nurses, doctors, corpsmen, and technicians whose sole wish was to make their plight better. They got clean sheets, hot showers, plentiful food (odd food, which we quickly supplemented with plentiful supplies of rice, a food they understood!), and remarkably advanced medical technical help. For many of them, for the first time in their lives they suddenly perceived that they had value as themselves, as individuals, as *someone*. They got a prayer room from a staff sympathetic to their religious needs. They got a play room where they could congregate and talk with each other, and where the children quickly learned to draw cute pictures of animals, stylized and fanciful portraits of the ship Mercy, boats, and frequently all too graphic depictions of what had happened to them and what they observed on shore. Of the gigantic tsunami seen from afar. Of the large trucks that gathered the dead and delivered them to mass burial sites. A picture of a ghostly presence rising from a cemetery, labeled in Bahasa "Dec 26, 2004; the day Banda Aceh died."

They had the chance to share all of this with each other, and share they did. People who arrived on the ship as strangers became family within hours. The children, injured and ill, smiled constantly and played with each other and with the medical staff, and were adopted immediately as family by all the other smiling Achenise people (as well as the entire staff of Mercy).

This closeness, this family-ness, if there is such a word, created some interesting situations.

Most everyone knows of HIPPA, the law that says each patient deserves total privacy of his medical records and conditions, and that no one else can be privy to that information without written consent, blah, blah, blah. Well, no had bothered to explain this concept to these people. When the doctors started making their rounds with an interpreter, they tried to do so according to HIPPA regs. That is, they separated the beds that the patients were in so privacy could be maintained and each conversation with the patient could only be heard by the attending physician, the interpreter, and the affected patient.

A problem immediately arose when the patients observed that they had a bed separated by several empty beds from the patient closest to them. How could they talk? How could they share stories of that horrible day, and about the wondrous care they were receiving aboard this giant white ship from these foreigners? So, they did the logical thing; they simply moved over several beds until they were within a few feet of each other. This was fine for chatting, but it really screws up things for those concerned with HIPPA and privacy and such.

So, from the first day on when the doctor and interpreter would appear, most able bodied patients and families would fall in immediately behind them as they went about their patient rounds. For a day or two, at most, the doctors tried to get the interpreters to explain to the hangers-on that they needed to converse with their patients *in private!* The gallery of observers would listen to the explanation with blank looks, then continue to follow the doctors as they went from bed to bed.

Now, none of us spoke Bahasa, so I expect it entirely possible that the interpreters were just saying, "Ignore these folks in white coats when they attempt to shoo you away. They must not have families where they come from. They'll get frustrated and leave you alone if you just stand there and do nothing." Or, something like that.

Because what happened was when the patient received bad news the assembled crowd would gather around them once the doctor had moved on and commiserate or pray, comforting the patient, accomplishing the emotional portion of the healing process far better than our efforts were likely doing. And, if the news were good they would all clap, smile, shake hands, and occasionally cheer, greatly adding to the delight and happiness of the patient receiving the good news.

All in all, I think I like their version of HIPPA better than ours!

Subject: Sitrep 9 Feb Banda Aceh

Today we decided to add some stress to the patient flow! 15 admissions from town, with excellent helo and comms support to accomplish this. Most of the patients are surgical, ranging from a hernia to massive tumors of the jaw, fractured mandibles, an open fracture of the radius, fractured femurs, and multiple others.

Several surgeries were carried out today, starting out at 0400 this morning when the radiologist and surgeon took the patient we received from the German hospital two days ago into the radiology suite and performed a very sophisticated and delicate procedure to block off an artery in the patient's stomach to stop profuse bleeding. The patient had suddenly bled out, losing about 1/4 of his blood volume. Their efforts were successful, but the effects of three prior surgeries before we received him, his chronic pancreatitis, and severe infection of his pancreas and other organs almost certainly dictate that he will not survive this. His wife has been counseled, and our staff is working intensely on him and with her.

Our other critical patient, the young boy who survived the tsunami and then had severe pneumonia and a respiratory arrest, is still critical. He is holding his own, barely, again with intense treatment by the infectious disease and pulmonary physicians, and constant attention from the nursing staff. Our young appendicitis patient who is the only surviving child of a family wiped out by the tsunami is doing great. The 14 year old girl (Machnawiah) whose arm we amputated yesterday is doing OK, but will have to have more surgery soon.

Other surgeries today included two difficult femur fracture repairs and a repair of an open complex fracture of the radius, as well as repair of a fractured mandible (jawbone). One of the femur fractures was on an 18 year old young man who gives a thumbs up and a smile to all of us who have taken part in his treatment. That is a little difficult to do, inasmuch as he has 2 broken arms and a broken leg from the tsunami, as well as losing his younger sister in that event. A great attitude; a brave young man. He makes us all smile when we work on him, as do most of these incredible folks. I'm not sure how they manage to do this, and I must note that it is humbling to all of us here.

1. 177 patients were seen at University Hospital today. Our efforts there are still somewhat chaotic, inasmuch as it is still a chaotic place with many moving and unconnected parts. However, with the aid of some extremely dedicated and sharp individuals ashore each day, people like CAPT Shela Norman and CDR Kurt Hummeldorf, as well as many others, our efforts are starting to

become more standardized and productive. As noted, 15 patients and 15 escorts were medevaced to the ship. We are going to have to hire more interpreters, and have some available locally to hire. We will proceed with that immediately.

2. Our outreach teams continue to work on water sanitation with UNICEF, and are working on performing some final assessments of the IDP (internally displaced persons) camps in Aceh. They visited with a water engineer from France, looking at a water distribution system. The French desire lab support for their water analyses.

3. The mental health team has their agenda outlined for the remainder of our time here.

They also met with UNICEF personnel, and are working on infrastructure development of program nodules to facilitate and renew mental care capacity for Aceh. There is a tremendous and unique opportunity for us here in this capacity.

4. We continue to receive multiple requests for more tours of Mercy, and for overnight stays for worn out NGO personnel. As soon as we accomplish the transition to CTF 73 (new command structure in charge of our effort), we will start working these issues.

5. We continue to supply oxygen to support the Operating Room and Emergency Rooms at University Hospital. We have 10 bottles to exchange tomorrow. The engineers' and medical technicians' reputations for wizardry at repairs are resulting in steadily increasing requests for assistance. They continue to rebuild motors, pumps, air conditioning units, refrigerators, electrical systems, etc. The ICRC hospital, run by the Norwegians, has requested that they come and help repair their X-ray unit.

6. I met with Dr. Rus today, along with Dr. Harold Timboe and Dr. Larry Ronan. Dr. Timboe and Dr. Ronan made proposals to Dr. Rus which he immediately accepted. Project Hope donors will work with the pulmonologist to build a state of the art pulmonary disease ward, concentrating on TB, which is endemic here. They hope to complete this task before Mercy departs the area. In addition, discussions were started to allow Harvard professors to come here for teaching purposes. Dr. Rus simplified the procedures for

allowing us to bring patients to Mercy for care, a task that is sometimes not easily accomplished under these circumstances.

7. Tomorrow we will send a 10 person maternal child team to Lamno. General Bambang, the senior TNI person in the district, will come to the ship for a visit, along with the Surgeon General and other members of the Ministry of Health. German helos may be available to start ferrying people and equipment to Mercy; they will work with Mercy tomorrow to accomplish this. We are sending 20 people to University Hospital tomorrow to assist in care. We are looking forward to the possibility of being allowed overnight stays there, inasmuch as this will greatly simplify lift requirements, and will allow greater flexibility to help out there.

We have 31 patients in the hospital now, and with the volume of surgery steadily going

up, probably will max out at about 40. We will continue to try to discharge patients in a timely manner. However, if this trend continues to go up, we may need increased number of nurses and corpsmen. In addition, if the flight schedule increases, consideration must given to augmenting the flight deck crew.

We are doing what we came here to do.

W. J. McDaniel

Subject: Sitrep 11 Feb Banda Aceh

Our little pneumonia patient who was found clinging to driftwood 2 km at sea continues to hold his own. While still critical, his blood studies are looking much better at this time.

The staff have sort of adopted him as a symbol; after going through what he has gone through, he should live. He frequently has not only a nurse at his side all night, but one of our pediatricians or infectious disease doctors as well. His lungs sound clearer now, and they will attempt to wean him off the respirator this weekend.

The other children have definitely come out of their reserved shells, and are like children everywhere; playing, laughing, and having fun. Our 4 year old burn patient who has straight legs for the first time in a long time insisted on being alone in the playroom for a while this evening so he could draw a picture for his favorite nurse.

We had VIP visitors from the Ministry of Health in Jakarta today, as well as a senior member of IOM and 3 personnel from Geneva representing WHO. They left after a good lunch and a tour of the facility, including the MOH (Ministry of Health) member talking with every patient in the hospital. (There are over 40 at this time.) She told me, "They like it here; everyone is so nice!" We discussed some proposed projects with the IOM physician and the WHO personnel, and will seek approval for those projects. We talked at length with them about our desire to not create a dependency on Mercy in Banda Aceh, but to work with them to quickly bring their facility up to the point where they can assume the care we are currently giving. They agreed with that concept.

EPMU6 presented their CONOPS plan to the leadership today.

1. We admitted 6 patients today, a mix of major orthopedic problems, tumors, and urological problems. We also brought 4 patients from shore to do cataract surgery. We discharged 3 patients.

2. 99 patients were seen ashore; dental again extracted considerably more teeth than they had patients.

3. Pharmacy inventoried and categorized over 700 boxes of medications today. The shelving they ordered has come in, and they found other shelving covered with mud; after a good cleaning it was serviceable.

4. Bio med worked on 2 X-ray machines all day.

5. Project Hope personnel met with the head of Pulmonology today and she presented the list of equipment she needs for a state of the art facility. Dr. Larry Ronan feels that the list is reasonable, and will proceed back to the states this week to try to purchase the items.

Agreement was reached on modifications and repairs to the existing facility she uses. She will have a state of the art pulmonary center, complete with isolation rooms for TB cases.

6. Dr. Rus, Director of Abidin (University) hospital wants to come to the ship for a visit as soon as he can arrange it.

7. All are hoping our CT scanner is repaired tomorrow when the technician gets here. There is a real need for its capabilities.

8. A team went to Lamno (a town an hour or so away) today and worked with the NGO's and Pakistani hospital there. The OB/GYN doctor saw 12 consults and arranged to meet with 20 midwives next Tuesday for discussions and examination of patients. 3 psych consults were done in conjunction with local psychiatrists. Arrangements were made for dental, ophthalmology, and urology clinics to be held soon.

9. There were 10 surgeries scheduled today, and a heavy load is anticipated tomorrow.

All in all, we are proceeding on schedule. Embassy personnel are aboard this evening attempting to guide us through the intricacies of local politics. After a long explanation from them, I have developed a headache. I am going to Jakarta tomorrow to meet with embassy personnel and NGO's there, returning to the ship on Tuesday.

W. J. McDaniel

As I have noted before, not everyone from our side wanted us there. This included a senior military officer at the embassy in Jakarta. He was not very receptive in my initial visit with him before arrival of Mercy, stating that the ship was not needed, the NGO's had plenty of medical help on the ground, and we were too late to do much good anyway.

He suggested that he could make a call or two and get the ship turned around, aimed at the West Coast of the United States instead of coming out and making his life more complicated. I had listened to his objections and complaints in silence, then finally tried a different line of reasoning.

"COL, let me try a straight forward explanation for our presence. First, the President...of the United States, that is...decreed immediately after the tsunami struck that we would deploy our state-of-the-art hospital ship to assist. The Secretary of Defense and the Secretary of the Navy immediately agreed that course of action was desirous, and soon thereafter the Chief of Naval Operations agreed with their thinking. The senior 4 star Admiral in the Pacific was placed in over-all charge of the operation and was the person in charge of deployment and operation of the ship; he was the person who hired me. Now, let me ask you a question. Do you think it is a career enhancing move for you to tell all of these rather distinguished gentlemen that their idea is dumber than dirt? Do you really see yourself winning that argument?"

Now, he did not achieve his rank and current position by being totally dense. He grudgingly conceded the logic of my argument, but was not happy

In the 3 weeks or so since I had visited with him in Jakarta he had continued to make snide comments in various communiqués to the ship and up and down the chain of command. On about 8 Feb he sent out a rather stupid message disparaging the wisdom of what we were doing, the effectiveness of our efforts, and several other observations in the same vein. I had had enough of his BS; we had a hard enough task to accomplish without having to listen to guff from our own personnel.

I sent the embassy an email stating that I was coming back to Jakarta and rather badly wished to chat with him; clearly we had a failure to communicate. So, Dr. Anne Peterson and I departed Mercy and flew to Jakarta.

I was met in the hotel there by his assistant who informed me that everything was all hunky-dory. The COL now understood what we were trying to do. I subsequently discovered that the Marine 3 star in over-all charge of the US relief efforts in the exercise had met with the COL in a closed door session for an hour or so. It seemed that no further discussions were needed. I actually never heard from that officer again, and certainly had no desire to have dinner or invite him for a game of bridge!

Anne and I made rounds again in Jakarta, visiting with and getting help from the embassy staff and USAID personnel. After several days we returned to Mercy.

Once back aboard the Commodore came to see me. I was told that I needed to call the 4 star Admiral in Hawaii. I did so.

"Where have you been?"

I told him.

"Why haven't you been sending in your situation reports?"

Well, I had no situation to report; I had been in Jakarta, out of touch with the daily activities aboard Mercy.

"Bill, I'm not going to bore you with identity of the senior folks who are reading those reports. You left us all hanging. What has happened to Iqbal? To the little girl whose arm you cut off? To all the others? What's their status? You just cut off in mid sentence and left everyone with no follow-up! Don't do that!"

I laughed; I really had thought that perhaps because my reports were in real language and not military jargon I might have just been irritating those folks who read them. If they read them at all. It seems that they were interested in the details, the *human* details, after all.

We discussed my further role in the effort. At that point I had accomplished what I had been sent out to do; that is, get all the approval needed to allow Mercy to work toward a successful conclusion, and find patients to be seen. I asked him if he thought I needed to stick around any longer.

There was a long silence.

"I think you should stay there; first, those daily reports, those human stories, need to keep flowing. And, more importantly, there are still all manners of things that we can't foresee that might come up. You work for me and are on the ground there; make sure those surprises that come up don't mess up what we are accomplishing there. So, yes, if you don't mind, stick around until the end of the mission."

Obviously I agreed with his reasoning. I was in the early stages of involvement of one of the most meaningful things I had ever done, and one that would affect my life (and almost everyone else involved as well) more profoundly than we could ever imagine.

Subject: Sitrep Banda Aceh 16 Feb

I returned from Jakarta today eager to find out what is happening new on Mercy. Well, lots. Patient flow continues at a high rate; we have seen over 1000 out patients and have done over 50 major surgeries since arriving. And, perhaps more important for the long haul, we have provided outstanding infrastructure building support for Abidin Hospital and other areas of Banda Aceh.

But, first, Iqbal. Iqbal is the young pneumonia patient who was found clinging to driftwood 2 km at sea after the tsunami. When I left here Saturday, he was still on a respirator and was totally non-reactive. Today, I entered to find him wide awake, breathing normally, bright eyed and smiling, literally encased in a pile of stuffed toys. He watched "Spiderman" last night and is now a big fan. He walked across ICU today, and went up on deck in a wheelchair with a big smile and big sunglasses on. He is a survivor. And, as you might imagine after having lived on tube feeding for the last several weeks, he has a ravenous appetite. He and his uncle are stars on our ship.

Our appendicitis patient has gone home with his father, the only member of his family other than him who survived the tsunami. Both were happy people when they left, but perhaps no happier than our staff who cared for them. My young barber who I visited professionally (from a barber standpoint) 3 weeks ago was operated upon Monday, and now has stable legs of equal length. He was most happy to see me, though he was looking rather critically at my ever-lengthening hair. And, not to make anyone squirm, a baseball sized stone was removed from a 18 year old fellow's bladder. No one here has ever seen one that size. Our 11 year old with a chest tumor, Jabal, has been diagnosed with a neurofibroma, a non-malignant tumor, but one which must come out. Mass General has offered to fly his father and him there free of charge for this complex surgery, but he will be evaluated tomorrow in Jakarta first.

By the way, the general consensus of the Indonesian workers is that the USA MRE's (meals ready to eat) are better than anyone else's.

1. We had 5 admissions today, and the hospital census is 38, with 7 in the intensive care unit. One of those is a young 7 year old girl similar to Iqbal; severe lung disease after being swept out to sea in the tsunami and inhaling lots of water. She has bilateral chest tubes in place at this time, and is in very serious condition. There were a total of 9 surgeries today, including 6 cataracts. 165 outpatients were seen, again with optometry, ophthalmology, and dentists seeing the vast majority.

2. We have 2 TNI physicians living on board now, greatly facilitating communications. Starting Monday, one of our physicians will start working in the TNI hospital each day.

3. Indonesian doctors continue to trickle back into Abidin Hospital, with 3 Indonesian surgeons returning today. They plan on resuming care immediately. Several Malaysian physicians will start working there soon as well. When surgical cases are contemplated for Mercy from this point on, one of the Indonesian surgeons will sign for the patient, and will hold them at Abidin if they can do the surgery. This is all part of our exit strategy, as we slowly back away while their capabilities increase.

4. Our outreach teams visited the County Health Clinic today; we are doing assessments there, and will help them procure a new steam sterilizer from IOM.

-They visited an IDP (internally displaced persons) camp with 1400 people in it. Interestingly enough, all those people came from the same village, and the population of the village was 2800 on the day of the tsunami. The 1400 survivors walked 13 hours to get to Banda Aceh. Again, our team was doing assessments of conditions, and found a number to report to IOM (International Organization for Migration) for repairs.

-The mental health team worked alongside UNICEF psycho-social team today. They will start an intensive course tomorrow reconstituting the mental health capabilities of the local mental health populace.

5. Engineering and bio-med repair has been extremely busy.

-They got the aeration pumps running at the water treatment facility today. They are in the process of trying to locate a pump for the facility, and will repair it if possible.

-They bought air conditioners and refrigerators for the pulmonary ward, and installed new windows, lights and screens.

-They managed to trace down the problems and repair the electrical grid, giving power to 4 or 5 new buildings in Abidin Hospital today. There was a possibility that they would need to dig up 900 meters of cable and replace it, but managed to trace the problem down and avoid this. In addition, they went to the Internet and found tech manuals for the air conditioners in several wards today, managing to repair 6 of them. The patients on one of the wards all gave them a big round of applause.

6. The Lamno (a town about 45 miles away) group brought a 25 year old, 24 week pregnant woman back to the ship. She has been having fevers since the tsunami, and needs an extensive workup.

Tomorrow will be a little lighter day; we have 4 major admissions planned, and with 7 patients in the ICU are about maxed out. We have several other surgeries we will avoid admitting until Saturday. Friday is a 'no fly' day, and will be spent doing surgeries and working on the patients we have. Saturday Dr. Winkenwerder (Assistant Secretary of Defense for Health Affairs) will be here all afternoon, making it a short day. 14 journalists will arrive Saturday, also. Sunday we will stand by in case POTUS (Presidents Clinton and Bush) drops by. No one seems sure if this will happen. Monday 15 Congressional staffers are coming, though no one on the ship is sure who they are; we may be unable to accommodate all their desires for lift, inasmuch as patient care does need to fit in here somewhere! We have a CODEL (Congressional Delegation) group arriving on Thursday.

I see no major let up in business in the near future. There is a question as to whether or not we will be allowed to go anywhere on the West coast other than here. Mark Llewellyn (Commanding Officer of the hospital aboard Mercy) and I are going to sit down with Dr. Rus on Saturday and plan a timeline on an exit strategy. If he wants us to hold to our original timeline of 19 March, we will be hard pressed to pull out much sooner. If not, that will not be a problem. I met the Indonesian Minister of Health on the plane from Jakarta today and talked with her. She expressed very sincere gracious thanks for Mercy's presence.

I continue to think the staff of Mercy has done an outstanding job. I hear praise from multiple levels as I travel about, and have had 2 ex-pats tell me, "Mercy makes me proud to be an American." The staff has managed to do this with considerable restrictions in place, such as the inability to remain on shore at night. While rumors are around about 'possible' security problems, there have been no incidents at all. We have followed the mandates dictated by GOI (Government of Indonesia) and TNI (Indonesian Army) to the letter, with nothing but positive results.

Bill McDaniel

I noted in this sitrep the return of some of the local host nation physicians. There was a real problem getting medical personnel back. First, about 1/3 of them had died in the tsunami. Then, the Indonesian government decreed that all medical care given would be free of charge. That's fine and dandy and seems to make sense, but unfortunately the host nation medical personnel at Abidin Hospital did not receive wages. The hospital was paid directly as they saw patients, ordinarily, and then paid wages to the doctors and nurses. With no income coming in by government decree, any returning medical personnel were forced to work without pay. And, most of them had lost part or all of their families and homes. Many of them left that part of Indonesia to live elsewhere with relatives and

67

friends, and practice medicine in an area where they could be paid for their efforts.

I sat down with Dr. Rus and discussed this problem with him. I asked him how much money it would take per month to pay his staff. He thought about it and came up with a figure of about $100,000.00/month needed. I told him I thought I might be able to get donations for that amount until they could start charging again. When I said I would try to get him the money he asked me to not give any to him or the hospital. Any income they received had to be turned over to the central health ministry in Jakarta, with them in turn dispensing back to the hospital what funds were needed. He said if I turned over a hundred grand to him he would be lucky to receive 1/10th of that in return. He asked if it would be possible for us to set up an independent money disbursing site? He would give us the names of the medical personnel and the amount of wages they should receive, and we would hand the money out. That way no money would need to be passed on to Jakarta.

This did present somewhat of a problem. Who could I find to act as a disbursing agent, and how much would they charge for the effort? And, frankly, who did I trust not to help themselves to some pocket change from the funds?

As I thought about this problem I went on my daily rounds to UN and NGO agencies I visited routinely. While sitting with the head of the UNICEF effort, an incredibly sharp woman, I asked her if she had any ideas about my problem.

"How much money are you trying to raise?"

I told her.

She shook her head and laughed. "Admiral, I have more millions of dollars than I know how to spend here. We could fund your effort with absolutely no problem, and the disbursing of funds could easily be done by my accounting folks. Will this help?"

Well, in a word, yes. So, Abidin Hospital started getting some badly needed medical help back, but slowly, slowly.

I mentioned in this sitrep our "Lammo" group. These were all female physicians and midwives, sent to Lammo to run an OB/GYN clinic. While in an emergency male physicians could see anyone, for routine care the Moslem faith really (I mean *really!*) preferred only females examining females. We luckily had a good group of nurse practitioners, midwives, and outstanding female physicians to accomplish this task.

Subject: Sitrep Banda Aceh 18 Feb

This was a no fly day, and the staff appreciated the rest. All except the ward personnel and operating room personnel got to stand down.

A few statistics to wrap up for two weeks work thus far. 284 teeth have been pulled. 660 X-rays have been taken, most of which are abnormal. A considerable number of them represent pathology which none of the staff on Mercy has ever seen before; some amazing cases. Over 1000 lab studies have been done, as well as 1600 prescriptions being filled. There have been 78 surgeries, most of which have been major. 5 of those cases were done today. We have seen well in excess of 1000 outpatients. About 1000 pairs of glasses have been fitted.

Finally, the effect of the infrastructure support we have given to Banda Aceh and to Abidin Hospital is almost impossible to accurately calculate. We are providing maternal child support, mental health support, water and sanitation evaluations, immunization teams to work with UNICEF, medical tech support, incredible engineering support, machine shop utilization to clean and rewire all kinds of engines and pumps, and miscellaneous support activities to multiple NGO's and UN activities.

Regarding on board patients, most continue to improve. No new patients were added, inasmuch as this was a no fly day. Betuin, the little 7 year old with big eyes, continues to be quite ill, and still has both chest tubes in place. Interestingly enough, her father who is accompanying her was coughing. We X-rayed him, and now he is under treatment for pneumonia. Mudasir, the barber, is improving steadily, though he has expressed a desire to stay aboard Mercy 'just a little longer.' A common desire. Iqbal, our miracle pneumonia save, is eating 'like a horse,' according to the staff. As I noted earlier, all the children appear malnourished. Iqbal is trying to remedy that in a few short days. He walked outside today, and will probably be going home early in the week. Our 14 year old with bone cancer and amputation of her arm had CT scans today. The radiologist biopsied two nodes to see if they represent metastases. Harvard is considering bringing her there for chemo therapy depending on the results of the ongoing studies.

Our last patient is a 9 year old girl with advanced glaucoma and bilateral cataracts. She was brought in yesterday in severe pain, and today had both cataracts removed. While this solved her pain problem, the question now is whether or not she will be able to see tomorrow when her bandages are removed. Glaucoma (greatly increased pressure inside the eyeball) will cause atrophy of the optic nerve if it is too high for too long. Her pressure was markedly elevated; the question unanswered at this point is whether or not it has been there too long. If so, she will have no vision at all. We won't know until her bandages are removed.

Tomorrow is a busy day. Almost 50 personnel are going ashore in a myriad of activities. CAPT Llewellyn, Dr. Timboe, and I are going to visit with Dr. Rus to discuss our suggested activities for the next 4 weeks. We will then return to Mercy to await the arrival of the Assistant Secretary of Defense (Health Affairs).

Bill McDaniel

My barber, whom I had met well before the arrival of Mercy, and who you might remember had a horrible limp secondary to an old unhealed fracture of the femur, was a delightful addition to the festivities aboard ship. And, there were festivities! The patients and staff interacted all the time, and there was always laughter on the wards, regardless of the seriousness of any patient injuries or illnesses. They were delighted to be there, and for most of them this was the first medical treatment they had ever received. The

Indonesian patients immediately became family to each other, sitting with each other, talking, visiting, caring for the children, and interacting (without a common language) remarkably with the hospital staff. The staff, military and civilian alike, seemed to thrive on the work and the interactions as well, though it seemed that we suffered our losses and failures far more grievously than the patients did. They had come to expect the worst and live with it; we never quite achieved that degree of acceptance.

Any patient who could do so "performed" if they could. My barber turned out to be an accomplished guitarist, and sitting in his wheelchair on deck would play and sing to a very attentive and appreciative audience. Machnaiwa, our delightful and beautiful 14 year old with osteosarcoma of the radius and on whom we had done a below elbow amputation, quickly became the organizer of all the other kids. Games, drawing competitions (the results of which were hung on display in the play room we had converted from a storage room), singing. She just constantly smiled and encouraged the other kids to do the same.

Fadhil, our little 4 year old who had come in with old burns and severe flexion contractures of his knees, and who had never walked, learned quickly when his contractures were released and his knees straightened. He had to hang onto something to walk, and delighted in the wheels on the portable EKG machine; they allowed him great mobility, and man, was he mobile! He would take off in a charge to run the machine into the nurses and doctors, laughing all the while as they laughed back at him.

All in all, a happy ship.

19 Feb 2005

We have been seeing patients actively for only 2 weeks now, but it feels like so much longer. For me it has been over 4 weeks, so maybe there is a reason it seems considerably longer. Project Hope personnel start rotating out next week, and I will follow them soon after that. My job was to prepare the way and do the political and personal things it took to get us accepted and enable us to see patients. (As noted before, I did not leave per the request of the Admiral who had hired me.) We are there.

I think everyone is getting so involved in their patients that it is going to be hard to let go. I can give an iron clad promise that everyone will remember them. You need to know Elisa, a 17 year old (who looks about 12) who was in the ocean with her mother for more than a day before she was rescued. Her mother died, but Elisa has survived, and has suffered the same malady that so many have suffered, tsunami lung. Terrible infections and pneumonia. In Elisa's case, she became hemiplegic, paralyzed on her left side. When she came to Mercy, she was miserable and withdrawn, and on CT scan a large brain abscess was found. She was started on aggressive IV antibiotic treatment, and is responding slowly, even smiling occasionally now.

Tonight the psychiatrist gave a lecture to the medical group on the grief process, relating it to the victims of the tsunami. It is possible that we might need to take that lecture a little more personally, however. After the lecture, a Project Hope emergency physician, versed in dealing with trauma and sick patients, stood up to make a comment about Elisa and her father's belief that her paralysis is because she has internalized her grief from her mother dying beside her. In other words, a conversion reaction. The physician started the story, then stopped, unable to continue. The room remained dead silent until he managed to take a few breaths and finally finish his story. No embarrassment in the room, however. Everyone in the room, and everyone on the ship who has dealt with these patients has felt the same way. No one will leave here untouched.

Our work continues the same as I have noted before. Lots of patients. Some of the most abnormal X-rays in the world. Tremendous strides in helping repair the infrastructure of Banda Aceh, including water and sanitation teams, engineering teams, immunization teams, mental health delivery, provision of oxygen to several hospitals when needed, and even delivery of a large bucket of ice cream to the Aussies, who work their butts off and are great friends to us. We took 5 pizzas into the University Hospital today for the emergency room and operating room personnel; they loved it. This is the most amazing pulling together of many countries, working alongside each other, that it has ever been my privilege to be a part of.

But, there is always a bottom denominator which colors our perceptions of everything. The Acehenise people. Unfailing politeness, courage, resilience, good humor, grace. What a delightful people! We are here to give them support, and I'm not sure who is getting more out of this exchange, them or us.

We have had many patients here, but perhaps none more symbolic than Iqbal, an 11 year old who was found clinging to a piece of driftwood 2 km out in the ocean many hours after the event. All of his immediate family had died, and his uncle found him 5 days later in a camp. Iqbal also suffered from tsunami lung, and slowly worsened. We got him about 2 weeks ago when he suffered a respiratory arrest at University Hospital. One of our helos was on the pad there turning, and we got him on a respirator on Mercy within an hour. He was totally unresponsive, had a white count of 80,000, had white lungs on X-ray. The infectious disease and pediatric doctors started working on him, with a doctor and a nurse staying by his bedside 24 hours a day. He was about the size of a 5 year old. We would all tiptoe in and look at him, waiting for...something. If anyone deserved to survive this, he did. Well, Iqbal was taken off the respirator one week ago, and today proudly sits in his bed in the middle of a pile of stuffed animals, smiling and watching Spiderman videos. He only quits smiling when he eats, which is frequently. He is trying to gain all those lost pounds back as quickly as he can. Iqbal is a survivor, and represents all that is good about these people here, to us.

Finally, a patient told one of our doctors at Abidin hospital through an interpreter, **"We are a very strong people. We take time to look ahead. We find time every day to laugh and some**

time to remember. Those of us who survive must live our lives, and we will be OK." I think they will.

Bill

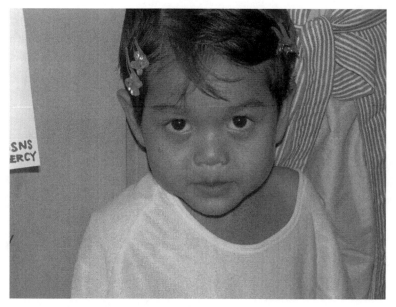

Uneasy patient awaiting evalutation

Chapter 6

THERE WERE ALWAYS dramas of some sort going on during this effort, as you might expect.

One day our education nurses went ashore to the TNI military hospital and spent the day giving classes on how to intubate patients and use a respirator to assist them in breathing. They had an extremely attentive audience of nurses and every available host nation physician in class, and at the end of the day left behind 3 respirators and intubation materials in case they were required. I'm sure we have all experienced receiving new equipment of some sort and immediately finding out that it actually might be of value.

That night 5 TNI soldiers were brought into the hospital in severe distress. They had been exposed to some noxious element and were all unable to breathe on their own. The night before it is likely that those soldiers would all have died. That night, however, the personnel managed to use their newly acquired skills and intubated all 5, managing their airways with respirators and hand-held Ambu bags until they were able to breathe on their own. When our personnel returned to shore the next day the staff of the hospital was quite proud of what they had accomplished, as they should have been!

Our surgeons went in daily to operate with the local physicians when complex cases came up that the host nation folk desired to handle in their facility. One day in the midst of a long and somewhat complex case all the lights went out; the generator had suddenly died.

No one panicked; nurses brought out flashlights and the last half of the case was completed without benefit of electricity. Their medical personnel was used to that and accepted it as a matter of course; needless to say, our personnel were a little more excited about the adventure! The result was a successful completion of the surgery.

We had become a common sight to the Indonesian people; they no longer looked upon us as oddities (at least not in an obvious manner). The landing site at the hospital usually had 40 or 50 interested onlookers around watching the comings and goings of the helos, and many Indonesians thronged the streets; after all, normal work was not on-going at that time.

One day as we were driving across to one of the NGO compounds I spied a small open front store, packed as usual with locals. I asked the driver to stop so I could run in and buy a couple of pounds of that incredibly rich Sumatran coffee. As I entered the store the 20 or 30 folks shopping there all turned and looked at me; after all, I was way bigger than them and certainly not a local.

Somewhat self-consciously I wandered around the store until I came to the shelves where several varieties of local coffee were stocked. A tiny little man who appeared to be about 80...but who might likely have been no older than me...planted himself in front of me, looking up at my face. He pointed at me.

"American?" He asked.

Well, interesting. Here I am, perhaps in somewhat hostile territory, being challenged by a tiny local. What to do? Answer in German. Try to appear Australian? I finally grinned at him and shook my head yes.

He threw his arms around me and hugged me, saying something to the others in the store. They all smiled and suddenly thronged around me. Seeing that I was trying to figure out what coffee to buy, I was abruptly besieged with advice from all sides...in Bahassa. While not understanding exactly what they were saying, the intent was clear. Each had his favorite coffee and wanted me to buy that one.

I wound up with considerably more coffee than I needed or wanted, but figured the other folks on the ship would appreciate it. So, I gathered my several pounds of coffee and headed to the cash register. As I approached it the same little old man suddenly appeared in front of me.

He tapped his chest. "I pay." And he did. When I attempted to pull my wallet out multiple voices demurred, indicating that I should leave it in my pocket. I left, bemused, touched, and aware that there might have been a sea shift in the attitudes that Americans were the "Great Satan." Maybe. Or, maybe they just sold me the worst coffee, not wanting me to get a taste for the good stuff. But I doubted that. I have thought about that brief encounter many times since that day.

One day I was asked if I would like to helo down to Meleuboh (about 125 miles away) , a town formerly of about 75,000 directly opposite the epicenter of the tectonic shifting plates that had spawned the tsunami. Meleuboh was a village on the coast and immediately rising several hundred feet into the surrounding hills, accounting for the sparing of some of its population. However, 40,000 of its 75,000 inhabitants had died. While I was there a couple of interesting events happened.

I was actually there accompanying several staffers from Washington, DC, who had come over to see what was going on, and I suppose report back on how the many hundreds of millions of dollars donated by Americans were being spent. As we drove around looking at the devastation the local populace was out vigorously trying to repair and rebuild.

One of the many after effects of the tsunami was that numerous fishing boats which had been anchored or tied up at the docks were washed inland until they nudged up gently...or not...against the hills. By the time the waters had receded the boats were high and dry in a grassy field about a quarter to a half mile from the new waterfront. I never did quite figure out where the old waterfront had been.

We saw a long line of men pulling on a large hawser rope attached to a sizable fishing boat in the field. It looked like heavy going! They were all pulling while men behind were pushing, and others were placing round logs under the keel; in spite of all the effort it appeared that little progress was being made. The staffers and I had all gotten out of the van and bought coconuts with straws in them from a local vendor; the local fast food equivalent, I suppose. The coconuts cost us about $.05 apiece, by the way. A lot cheaper, and somewhat more tasty, than the $1.79 diet Coke I buy at home.

There were a few other folks watching the on-going effort in the field; one was a Caucasian woman. As we watched the sweating men slowly inch the boat across the grass we turned and looked at the shoreline in the distance; as far as it looked to us, I felt sure the men hauling on that craft thought it looked an impossible distance away.

The staffers were used to American power, American capabilities, and plentiful American money.

The senior staffer observed, "Someone needs to tell them they will never get that boat to the water. They should wait and maybe we can find a truck that might be able to pull it for them."

A female observer glanced over at us.

"Gee, I wouldn't tell them that. You might make them feel badly about the 30 or 40 other boats they have already managed to get out of that field to the water." She turned away from our group and continued to observe. As it turned out she was one of the USAID personnel who had provided the wages for the men to get all those boats back in the water, giving them badly needed funds and letting them be a direct part of the rebuilding of their town. No, they didn't need no stinking trucks!

As the staffers were off getting briefed by someone I wandered around and came upon a large blue tent with "UNICEF" on the sides. I asked my interpreter what the tent was? Well, it was a tent to provide care for the orphans left when over half the population of the city had died. I told him I wanted to look in.

As we approached the tent I could hear children inside; shrieking, laughing, and making other playing noises common to all children everywhere. I stepped into the tent where probably 15 or so adults were assembled along with 50 or 60 playing kids. They had toys and games and adults attempting to organize some efforts, and were clearly having a ball. Yep, many of their parents and brothers and sisters had died a few weeks earlier, but they were kids and had each other and infectious laughter. That combination could not be equaled by a dozen highly qualified psychiatrists.

I had my camera with me and started to take some pictures. A small crowd of little boys spied the camera and immediately gathered in a half circle in front of me hamming it up. I laughed and continued to take pictures of them. I noted a girl, maybe 10 or so, trying to get past the boys into the front of the circle. She elbowed her way forward until she was directly in front of me; her progress was somewhat hampered by the resistance and resentment of the boys who did not want to be displaced. As she planted herself in front of me several of the boys made comments to her in Bahassa. She turned and slowly glared at each of them in turn, turned her head back toward me, and delivered some sort of definitive statement to them.

My interpreter laughed. "Admiral, do you want to know what she said?"

I said, "Let me see if I understood her. I think she said something like, 'You're just a bunch of stupid boys!' "

The interpreter's mouth dropped open. "You understand Bahassa?"

I laughed. "No, actually, I don't. But I grew up with four sisters, and have seen that look so many times I just figured it had to mean the same thing in Bahassa as it did in English."

Non-verbal communication can be quite effective at times!

As I started to leave the tent a twelve year old very pretty little Achinese girl walked over to look at me. She had her ten month old brother in her arms, a little roly-poly kid with round cheeks and a smile. He looked up at me and suddenly held out his arms. I took him as the interpreter explained to the girl who I was and what I was doing there. Meanwhile the baby was observing me closely. Smiling contentedly he reached out to grab my sunglasses and settled in like he intended to spend the afternoon relaxing by a pool. My heart truly did feel like it was melting as the interpreter told me their parents had died on December 26, 2004. I held him as long as I could; someone took my camera and snapped a picture. I still feel a marked tug at my heart when I look at that photo; what has happened to those two children today? The most likely thing, of course is that both have been taken in by distant relatives; there are few real orphans in Indonesia. Any known relatives lay claim to the survivors and make them a part of their family. A wonderful tradition, I think.

There were other dramas of our own making. When so many folks are involved in an endeavor, and many of those vitally interested folk many thousands of mile away, there will be decisions made occasionally that, while well intentioned, are just not quite right!

I've noted before the moderate discussion about the possible security problems (presence of the GAM rebels) that might have existed at that time in Sumatra. This had resulted in our not being allowed to leave personnel ashore at night, even in secure compounds run by the UN. While that might have decreased our efficiency and created some communication problems, we lived with the restrictions and worked around them. I certainly understand the desire of higher authorities in the US to keep all our personnel safe; shoot, we liked that attitude! However, the TNI and UN continued to assure us that there were no security concerns at that time.

One Wednesday evening the Commodore and hospital Commander approached me and told me that beginning Saturday our security personnel who had been accompanying us to shore daily would start carrying concealed weapons.

I reacted rather negatively. "Commodore, that is specifically against the Status of Forces agreement that all the countries here are observing. Weapons are not allowed on shore. If we do that, and get caught, it could jeopardize our entire mission here and abruptly terminate the good will we seem to have generated. You need to tell whichever higher authority that told you to do this that it is not a good idea. In fact, you are the senior active duty person in theater; tell them absolutely not!"

The Commodore looked uncomfortable. "Admiral, I will try again on the VTC (video tele-conference) tonight to discourage this."

I replied, "You're the man. You can make it happen. And, if for some reason you can't, I think I can." I thought perhaps a subtle threat might be of some value. Probably not, though.

The next evening the hospital CO approached me. "Admiral, I just thought I would let you know that the Commodore pleaded our case tonight, but was overruled. He was told that regardless of his desires to the contrary, on Saturday our on-shore security would start carrying weapons."

Well, hell! How stupid was this?! We had no credible threat, and that was based on daily contact with the TNI and other knowledgeable folks ashore. We were well on the way to possibly establishing an outstanding relationship with these folks. And, if we were found with weapons ashore, or even worse, one of our personnel actually used his weapon, we would lose all the good will and probably be evicted from the country! Why someone, somewhere, decided on this course of action was beyond me, and definitely failed any common sense validation I could come up with.

It was 10:30 PM, and I picked up the phone to call Hawaii. Suddenly, I realized that the senior person in the Pacific theater outside of Hawaii was the Commander 7th Fleet in Yokosuka, Japan. I had worked for 7th Fleet in 1984-86 and knew that the Commander was usually an unusually sharp Admiral, almost always destined to achieve his 4th star and be one of the Navy's highest leaders. I figured that I owed that person the courtesy of discussing this problem before I went to the 4 star.

I called the flagship of the 7th Fleet, USS Blue Ridge, at pier side in Yokosuka. When they answered I asked them to ring the 3 star for me.

The command center Officer of the Day said, "Sir, are you aware it is 0030 in the morning, and the Admiral is surely asleep." I assured him that I was aware of that, but requested that he put the call through.

A sleepy 3 star answered. I told him who I was (we had never met) and explained the problem. "Admiral, I have no idea who ordered this, but I am sure it is someone between your office and this ship. We just can't allow this; we can't violate the Status of Forces agreement and thereby jeopardize our efforts here."

He was silent for a moment, then explained that inasmuch as he had just awakened (a subtle jab there), perhaps he had misunderstood me. Would I repeat what I had just said? I did so.

He exploded. "You have no idea where that order originated?" I assured him that I did not.

"Bill, I will get to the bottom of this and get back to you."

About two hours later I received a call from the Admiral again. Problem solved. There would be no weapons carried ashore. I never did know who had ordered this, but am sure they regretted having done so. (On the other hand, I also am absolutely sure that that individual had the best interests of our personnel at heart. Just a decision that, no matter how carefully thought out, was the wrong one at that time.)

I recently had the occasion to meet that 3 star; he is now the Chief of Naval Operations and runs the Navy. When I reminded him about the above incident, he asked if he had solved the problem. I assured him he had done so!

Lots of professionals dealing with lots of big problems. Sometimes things can go awry in spite of our best intentions. And, sometimes not.

Before I truly finish this tale I hope to return to Indonesia and find out what has happened to many of the remarkable people I was honored to encounter during the three months I was there.

Faces of the Tsunami

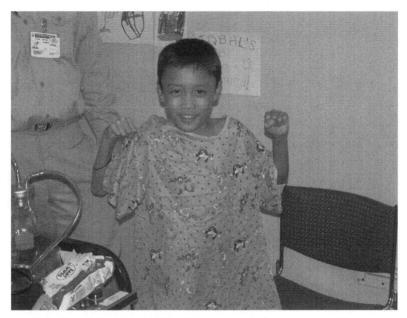

Iqbal making a muscle after two weeks on a ventilator

Chapter 7

Subject: Sitrep Banda Aceh 20 Feb

TODAY WAS A LIGHT day; we had two Presidents in the area, and had to be a ready platform for them. A light crew went into Banda Aceh. Upon arrival in the Emergency Room at Abidin University Hospital, 2 of our nurses noted a severely ill young man in the rear of the ER, unattended except by a hysterical family. Further enquiry revealed that the patient, an 18 year old man, was hit on his moped sometime last night, then placed in the back of a pickup and driven several hours to Banda Aceh. The emergency personnel felt that they could do nothing for his condition, which was critical. His only chance, and a very slim one it is, was Mercy. The nurses recognized immediately that if we did not act swiftly he would die. In spite of no fly regulations due to the Presidential visits, they ordered a helo and the patient was transferred to Mercy. He is virtually beyond critical, with a fractured femur, fat emboli in both lungs, aspiration pneumonia in both lungs, ARDS (adult respiratory distress syndrome), and an apparent sub-arachnoid (brain) bleed. It is highly unlikely he will survive. However, when CAPT Llewellyn and I checked in on him a few minutes ago, there was a team of some of the top critical care doctors in the country around his bedside. Five of them, actually. They will be there all night, and will remain until he either starts recovering, or not. His father is nearby, and understands fully the gravity of his son's condition. He also understands that the only chance his son has is to be exactly where he is.

Only 15 patients were seen by specialists at Abidin today. The Australians have offered as many of their nurses as we need to help us cover the gap between the departure of Project Hope personnel and the arrival and orientation of the new Project Hope crew. They will likely start coming out immediately for this cooperative venture. Again, I think everyone will benefit from this arrangement. This is just another example of the incredibly positive value of having this ship here, and of having an intermixing of highly qualified military and civilian personnel caring for the patients in this floating hospital.

In discussions with Dr. Rus at Abidin Hospital today, he stated that one of his big needs is for the large fence around the hospital to be rebuilt for security. The mud and water flow just flattened it out. In addition, his staff has no place to live. He hopes to get barracks built for them, inasmuch as real estate prices have gone up so much since the tsunami (due to the influx and payments from foreigners) that none of his staff can afford to live nearby in private residences.

Finally, none of his staff has received any pay since the tsunami. In normal times they charge for treatment and for hospitalization, but the government has decreed that all care will be free. He is struggling to figure out where he can find money to start paying wages again. Until this happens, he will have great difficulty finding adequate numbers of staff to return. (I find it an odd thing that so much money has been promised to Indonesia for problems caused by the tsunami, but none has found its way toward this end.)

Tomorrow we will send out in excess of 50 personnel to work in the community. I will travel to Meleuboh with the congressional staffers coming in to look at possible needs there, after conferring with the TNI locally in Meleuboh.

If anyone has any ideas on how we might be able to direct funds toward those needs noted above, we would appreciate suggestions. I realize that this is not our problem, but it just seems that somehow there must be a way to guide funds to the right place.

Bill McDaniel

As you can readily note, several of the problems noted in this sitrep were resolved shortly thereafter. It's interesting to compare what can be done through all the "official" sources and what can be done much more readily through contacts and friendships. In my work in various Asian countries, I have found that personal relationships are not only more conducive to getting things done than contracts and official channels, but are in fact absolutely necessary.

Subject: Sitrep Banda Aceh 21 Feb

First news first. The 18 year old young man we brought in yesterday and who had a gathering of outstanding doctors gathered around him all night last night is doing much better. Certainly not out of the woods yet, and still critical. But, he lived through the night, and his clinical signs continue to improve. Just goes to show that it pays to be 18 years old, and it pays to accidentally wind up in a place with the most outstanding doctors and nurses anywhere. You gotta be a little lucky. He is, and we hope he stays that way.

We discharged 9 patients today. Finally! The wards have been full. ICU is still busy, but the patient numbers are manageable now. We had only 2 admissions today, a femur fracture (seems like one a day), and an abdominal tumor. We sent 49 folks ashore today, and returned 58. This included 3 Aussies and 6 USAID and HAC staffers. We did 5 major surgeries on board.

1. 244 outpatients were seen at Abidin Hospital, including giving out 186 pairs of glasses.

2. 4 people were brought from Abidin for out-patient CT scans. 3 were returned.

3. 2 TNI (military) oral surgeons will join us tomorrow for 7-10 days of working with our surgeons. In return, we will send one doctor and one nurse to the TNI hospital daily.

4. Engineering fixed the diesel generator motor at Abidin hospital today; this is the first time it has run since the tsunami. Engineering also bought an air conditioner with donated funds and installed it in the pharmacy today, preventing the meds from ruining in the heat, and making the pharmacist's life somewhat more tolerable than before.

5. Mr. Bill Yeager, special envoy from Ambassador Pascoe to Banda Aceh for reconstruction efforts reported that for the last several days he has visited many folks on shore, and that "everyone" knows Mercy is here and loves the support we give.

6. Our nursing staff starting teaching at the nursing school in Banda Aceh today, and were met with great enthusiasm by the 60 nursing students.

7. Pharmacy reports that all shelves have been purchased and installed. Our pharmacist and tech are in the process of separating all the meds.

8. Public health personnel met with UNICEF and worked toward a comprehensive teaching program. They will present 150 pages of our material to an audience, who will then teach 1200, then reach out to an estimated 50,000 persons in Aceh province. This is force multiplication.

-Several teams went out to several district IDP camps today and inspected them for improvements to be performed by UNICEF. Lots of deficiencies were identified. In the course of the visits, several thousand stuffed toys were distributed.

9. RDML Vanderwagen went to the Health Sector meeting today and updated them on
Mercy's activities since arriving. His report was received with 'great satisfaction.' The Ministry of health wants a copy of our activities.

-A new round of measles and cholera vaccinations will begin next week, and we will provide teams for that activity.

10. CAPT Llewellyn and I met with Dr. Rus today. He is quite apprehensive about us leaving at the same time the Germans are departing. The Australians left today. He is still struggling to get his surviving staff back to work.

-I went to Meleuboh today and met with the senior UN official there. She seemed quite excited to see a representative of Mercy, and is to send me an email outlining all she wants to work with us on. She expressed several times that she was thrilled that we were in the area. The harbor master will send us data about the harbor there.

-The area in Meleuboh was devastated, though not as completely as Banda Aceh. It is still extremely impressive. All the residents apparently ran out after the earthquake to check on each other, and the wave, estimated to be 22 meters high and traveling at an incredible speed, hit them, killing virtually everyone it its path. I visited a Childrens' Center, where all the children, and there were many, had lost at least one parent in the tsunami. They were delightful and irrepressible.

Finally, I was riding around with a young (30 or so) Australian who has been here since the first days. He said that a couple of weeks ago he started having bad nightmares about what he had seen. He went to see a counselor who is there for staff help, and told me that the counselor explained that his nightmares were just reflecting what he had seen, and were his mind's way of coping with the disaster. In practical Aussie style, he noted, "Once he explained that, it made sense to me. So, I quit having those dreams." If it were only that easy for all these folks.

Bill McDaniel

As I have noted before, the Australians were on the scene before almost anyone else, and were indefatigable in their work. It was primarily them who had to sift through the deep mud in Abidin hospital and dig out the several hundred bodies, many of whom were kids. Yep, they had nightmares; they had definitely earned them.

By this time Mercy had been on the site for 3 weeks or so, and the system put into place was working smoothly. After the first rough few days, helos were always available, the evening meetings to establish priorities for the next day were well attended and orderly, medical and engineering staff went ashore every day. They worked diligently while the surgical staff and ward nursing staff aboard ship remained exceedingly busy, with 4 operating rooms running 12-18 hours/day.

We had lots of very knowledgeable experts in many subjects aboard ship, so in the evenings we had a series of outstanding educational talks given by various personnel. And, the galley kept putting out superb meals, augmented about once a week with ice cream...a real treat in this climate! '

Before the first group of Project Hope personnel rotated off the ship we had a sizable "steel beach" picnic, replete with hot dogs, hamburgers, ice cream, cookies, and cake. Plus the standard number of sunburns. After all, most of our folks were isolated below decks most of the time, and there was an awfully lot of skin just waiting for a decent burn. Patients who were able...and many we had to carry...were encouraged to come out for the picnic. They loved it; in fact, most had probably never done anything remotely like this.

Most days I went ashore to continue to communicate with all interested parties. It's fascinating to me how fast things can fall apart by the simple lack of communication. Not that anything significant has changed; just natural paranoia arising, I suppose. Regardless, a strong lesson learned from this entire effort is that there cannot be too much communication. Daily communication heads off the problems before they become so, and finds solutions almost before solutions are needed. I think this is one aspect of our military disaster relief work that we do not do well. (After the recent Haiti earthquake we responded in a major way, as everyone knows. And, we saved many lives. However, on the ground in Haiti we did not do a very good job of coordinating and communicating. I received a disappointing email from the same senior WHO woman I had worked with in Banda Aceh. She asked what had happened since Banda Aceh? They could see our hospital ship sitting at the pier, but did not know the rules. Some patients were accepted, some rejected, and she had no idea why. And, she was unable to get onto the ship to get clarification. I'm sure the folks aboard ship were busting their butts working day and night. But, it just takes one person dedicated to keeping the lines of communications open to resolve misunderstandings and problems before they reach a critical mass.) As we continue to respond in the future to disasters around the world, this should be a process of continual improvement...I hope.

Subject: Sitrep Banda Aceh 22 Feb

Some updates on old friends. Iqbal, the 11 year old who came in with severe tsunami pneumonia and looked to be almost dead, is still going strong. He is about the size of a 7 year old, and almost impossibly skinny. He has been eating 6 meals a day since coming out of his coma 10 days ago, and has gained 10 pounds in the last week. He is out walking daily, weakly, but smiling through it all. I took a picture of him today, and he 'flexed' his arms aka Superman. Hard to do when your biceps are only about 4 inches around.

We have another delightful young girl in, about 4, who is going to undergo a kidney removal. As are the others, she is shy and quiet, but smiles easily. Elisa, our 14 year old with a post-tsunami pneumonia and brain abscess, was returned to the ICRC hospital today for continued IV antibiotics. She is one of the first two patients I saw almost a month ago.

The other, Jabal, is at the TNI hospital in Jakarta, but we are hoping he will be allowed to be treated at Mass General. He has a huge neurofibroma inside his chest cavity. (His transfer to Mass General did not happen. Jabal's father desperately wanted him to be taken to the US for treatment. This was an extremely complicated case, and without exacting surgery he would have an unstable spine and a resultant paraplegia. The TNI were insistent that they could do the necessary surgery. The father came to me and we had a long talk via an interpreter. Finally, the father shrugged his shoulders in disgust and said, "It's all politics." He was quite perceptive. I would love to know how Jabal ultimately fared. Or, maybe I wouldn't.)

Another young 7 year old I mentioned last week with bilateral chest tubes and pneumonia from tsunami lung has been slowly improving. Unfortunately her father and she had to transfer back to Abidin Hospital. All the rest of her family had been killed in the tsunami except for 2 brothers. They were placed in an IDP camp when her father brought her out to Mercy, and have gone among the missing. The father wanted to take her back to Abidin so other extended family could watch over her while he looks for her brothers. It is a different world out here.

Our little 14 year old with an amputation of her left arm for bone cancer continues to be one of the ship favorites. Because of her metastases, it is highly unlikely that any further treatment would be of benefit to her. With her incredible smile, it's tough on everyone to realize that she will probably never live to age 20. She has contributed at least half of the drawings in the play room. We are cataloguing those drawings carefully. (Hopefully if I ever publish this book I will be able to have several pages devoted to those well done, and some very disturbing, images.)

Because of mechanical problems, we had only one helo available today. It did a lot of work!

1. We saw 129 outpatients ashore today, and while there ophthalmology did 12 cataract surgeries. They are doing lots of people lots of good. 83 pairs of glasses were handed out, and 19 teeth removed. (By dental, not ophthalmology!)

2. We did 8 ICRC CT scans aboard today. We also had 3 Aussie doctors who spent last night aboard, and will spend tonight here as well, due to available lift being fully employed today.

3. We continue to have lots of folks who would like to visit Mercy; lift constraints prevent many of them from coming on board at the moment.

4. Outreach teams continue to work with UNICEF, and evaluated 3 IDP camps today.

They continue to find lots of deficiencies, which they report and which are then corrected by UNICEF.

5. A Project Hope pediatrician and a team evaluated another IDP camp with 274 adults and 68 families in it today. All the families were fishermen, but have no boats from which to fish anymore. However, he noted that the 28 year old village elder was extremely courteous and thanked them for inquiring about his people's health. As usual, they were dignified and polite. His statement: "It's so nice that you ask how we are doing."

6. Psychiatry outreach is continuing to work on their week's program of reaching ultimately 50,000 folks with their programs. They have 5 people doing the interface.

7. The Australian nurses and techs will arrive tomorrow morning to work aboard the ship to supplement our change of Project Hope nurses.

8. CAPT Holzinger has 60 cataract surgeries scheduled, and more are coming daily.

9. Tomorrow 43 folks will go ashore. All the EPMU pallets are ashore now.

10. We are building up a large case load ashore awaiting surgery. The screeners will start prioritizing the surgeries. Almost all are huge surgeries.

We are awaiting word from the UN camp at Meleuboh to see which outreach teams we might need to send to assist there, security conditions permitting.

We continue to be gainfully employed here in Banda Aceh, and there is little doubt that we could be thus employed for the foreseeable future. However, we will start the delicate process of slow disengagement within 7-14 days, hoping to send more and more of our surgeons ashore to operate with the local surgeons, rather than continuing all surgeries aboard ship. The outreach teams should be able to continue working ashore at a full pace right up to the time we depart the area on 16 March. We will have to coordinate closely with the area hospitals, and rounds will need to be made during the week prior to departure to get readouts from the various agencies as to how they have seen our assistance.

This continues to be one of the most rewarding experiences any of us have ever participated in.

Bill McDaniel

All in all, while we did an incredible amount of work both ashore and on board Mercy, the teams who probably touched more folks than anyone were dental, eye, engineering, and psychiatry outreach. This always seems to be the case. Surgery is sexy. Fixing cleft palates makes for great pictures and helps the individual affected. However, as far as touching many lives for years in the future repairing dental and eye abnormalities and deficiencies are probably the two most far-reaching activities we can be involved in. It has been this way in virtually every disaster relief or humanitarian assistance program I have ever been involved in.

As we approached the Indonesian imposed deadline for most of the external help leaving the country (March 19), there continued to be an increasing urgency on the part of patients ashore to be seen and fixed if possible. After all, I think most of the incredibly delightful Indonesians we were seeing had never seen a doctor before this. Word spreads quickly. People showed up for evaluation for conditions that were sometimes amenable to treatment, but in many cases were far beyond anyone's capabilities. And yet, these gentle people would hear the bad news and miserable prognosis with grace and tranquility, gently touching their heart and their head has they bowed and murmured, "Terumi casi." Thank you.

And leave to calmly face their fate.

First Project Hope crew of health care workers

Chapter 8

Subject: Sitrep Banda Aceh 23 Feb

TONIGHT WE SAID goodbye to the first half of our first group of Project Hope doctors and nurses; the second half will leave on 28 Feb. We have 90 more coming in to replace them. However, we all are losing most valued friends when this crew leaves. The events of the evening were touching, and most of us at one time or another expressed what we all thought: "Can't you all stay for the next 3 weeks?!" What an amazing crew. And, they will leave a significant part of themselves behind.

Our little four year old burn victim who now has straight legs is almost impossible to get to smile...except when one of the Project Hope volunteer social workers is with him. He smiles and laughs all the time then. His aunt told us through an interpreter, "I have never seen him do that! I don't believe that is my nephew!" The next crew in will be just as good, and will do a great job, and when they leave on 19 March, we will miss them as well. But tonight, we do hate to see this professional bunch go.

Iqbal, our tsunami pneumonia survivor, went home today. It was time, and he, more than anyone, represents these people to us. As I noted 2+ weeks ago, if anyone deserved to live, he did. And, due to his incredible resilience and resolve, and to simply the best medical care available anywhere, he will go on to his future.

I mentioned our 7 year old pneumonia patient who had to be moved back to Abidin hospital yesterday so her father could try to find his sons. He had lost his 3 other daughters and his wife in the tsunami, and could not bear to lose the two boys. Another patient's relative here on Mercy went to the hospital and stayed with the daughter, and today Dad found his two sons.

Our 18 year old moped accident victim who was almost dead when he came here 60 hours ago is doing well. Tomorrow we will take him in and rod his femur; he is still sedated, and we still do not know if he suffered any brain damage. Again, no better medical care could have been rendered anywhere.

Finally, we are seeing some of the most incredible pathology any of us have ever seen, and much of it tragic. We had a 14 year old boy come in today, and on CT scan was literally filled with cancer. No treatment possible. We removed two kidneys today, one from a delightful 7 year old girl. Her diseased kidney was the size of a bowling ball. Again, I don't know why, but at least it was not malignant. She should have no further problems from that source.

1. We did 8 surgeries today, making an even 100 done here since 3 February. All have been major, and some of a nature no one here has ever seen. The orthopedic surgeons have been the most gainfully employed, cheerily rodding femurs and tibias as quickly as they can grab the next hammer. (When they run low on patients we intend to send them into help rebuild the hospital. They won't even have to change instruments.) We admitted 5 patients, plus 5 attendants. We sent 12 home today.

2. We welcomed 10 Aussie nurses and corpsmen aboard today; they will help us for the next few days in staffing the wards. They have already shown that they are highly skilled, and have been absorbed into the routine of the ship smoothly.

3. Optometry saw 250 patients ashore today, prescribing glasses for every one of them. Total patients seen by all ashore was 307, and ophthalmology did 13 surgeries. Dental saw 25 patients, pulling 86 teeth. (I'm not sure why that statistic seems interesting; we all demand to know the number of teeth vs. patients. Morbid curiosity, I suppose; we all carefully check our own teeth while they are reporting.)

4. Our military Moslem chaplain went ashore today and was welcomed. The local folks want him to come ashore in the future in uniform. They feel that showing that he is an American and a Moslem will have a very positive effect on the attitude of the people in the IDP camps toward Americans. He brought back 3 local translations of the Koran for the patients aboard ship, and will return to the IDP camps as much as possible in the future.

5. 2 nurses and a physician went to the TNI hospital today. The nurses helped educate the ICU nurses in a 4 hour class there, and have been requested to return each day to help
them further their education. The TNI would like at least one, and preferably 3,
physicians to come daily to assist them.

6. Mental health is in the midst of their UNICEF project, one with an incredibly high payoff. This is one of the more far-reaching and valuable efforts we have been involved in. NHK TV from Japan was there filming them today.

7. RDML Vanderwagen and team went to IOM today, to find that the EPMU6 team is settled in and working hard. Their lab is set up and functional. HHS is working some long term projects with the Indonesians in several areas.

-One thing noted was that the NGO's in town, over 150 of them, are largely pursuing their own objectives, regardless of Indonesian desires. There is little coordination, a common complaint heard from the UN agencies. The US Public Health Service is one of the few that is trying to remain totally coordinated with the UN toward future goals. He has been told that the Indonesians see us as responding to their needs and desires, and not pursuing ones of our own.

8. The engineers remain busy, and repaired a ventilator today. They also continued work on a children's ward, and are supporting a new electrical team with cabling, fuses, and the like.

-They note that Abidin hospital has no infrastructure support teams, no repair teams, no intrinsic ability to effect any medical repairs. They do not know what they will do for this when the foreign workers depart.

9. Dr. Rus' deputy from Abidin came to the ship today and spent all day with us. CAPT Llewellyn and I were with him throughout the day. He was extremely impressed with Mercy, and bemoaned the lack of staff at Abidin. He said the situation where the doctors cannot charge anything (by government decree) was driving many of them to other islands so they can continue to make a living. They have about 45 general doctors, 30 specialists, 150 nurses, and assorted techs. All are getting minimal or no money. We asked him what it would take to pay them per month, and the figure is about $100,000/month at a minimum for all. He said if they could get 3 months wages they think they could entice many of them back into the hospital. Of interest, he noted that if the money were given directly to the hospital administration, most of it would have to go to Jakarta. The only way all the money could stay locally would be for someone to sit up a private entity to just pay the wages directly. (As noted earlier we managed to help solve the pay problem.)

-We discussed in some detail plans for Mercy to slowly phase out of Banda Aceh. Starting Sunday some of the specialists will start coming to Mercy to visit and talk with our specialists. We will start sending our physicians in to operate with them at Abidin in selected cases, and our non-surgical physicians will start making rounds and consulting at Abidin. Our nurses will start working along side their nurses, not replacing them. We will slowly decrease the number of admissions on Mercy in this manner. A lot of attention will have to be paid to equipment used; we will likely have to carry some ashore for the effort.

10. We are spending more and more time working on the future movements of the ship, along with many people reading this sitrep, I'm certain. I plan on going to CTF 73 for a couple of days in early March, then on to Jakarta to the Embassy for a couple of days discussing our plans for now and the future.

Finally, there was a long interview in the Jakarta paper today with CAPT Mark Llewellyn. One of the interviewers asked Mark how we got along with so few interpreters? How did we manage to communicate with the patients in these instances? Mark's reply: "We talk from our hearts to their hearts."

Tomorrow is a light day as we trade out Project Hope personnel.

Bill McDaniel

The CTF is the Commander Task Force, a 3 star Marine General stationed in Pattaya Beach, Thailand.

The Project Hope medical personnel who had been ashore for the initial three weeks of the deployment were deeply involved and committed, and virtually all wished they could stay longer; in fact, a few extended, losing their stateside jobs in the process. Everyone I talked with told me that the three weeks they had been involved with the patients of Indonesia were the most rewarding days of their lives.

On their last night on ship we had a large meeting of all personnel in the wardroom (lunchroom). The Project Hope personnel were honored by many of us in brief talks. All during the time they had been on board I had heard repeatedly the sentiment, "How do you folks do this? Why stay in the Navy and be deployed and on board ship all the time?

Don't you miss your families?"

That night I asked the Project Hope folks to stand and look toward the back of the room where the medical personnel of Mercy were assembled, including officers and enlisted personnel.

"Many of you have asked how the Navy personnel can do this, and yet almost all of you have told one or the other of us these three weeks have been the most meaningful of your lives. Well, look at those folks standing and sitting in the back of the room. Why do they remain month after month and year after year? It's not for the money, nor for the ability to remain in one place with family and have a stable economic and school situation. They remain because what you refer to as the most momentous 3 weeks of your lives *is* their lives. This is what they train for. This is what they get the opportunity to do repeatedly year after year. By and large, this is what keeps us in the Navy. We feel like we are part of a larger picture; the good feeling you have had while here is one we get to repeat over and over again. That's why we stay."

Subject: Sitrep Banda Aceh 24 Feb

A quiet day. Today was a change out day for Project Hope, so only ten people went ashore. The helos did an outstanding job of ferrying a total of 74 people back and forth to the airport, plus a couple of lifts of luggage. There were no admissions or discharges.

There were five surgeries today, including two angiography cases in the Operating Room. The little girl who had a kidney removed yesterday has a temp, but seems to be doing well. The 18 year old who was in a moped accident and who we did not think would survive had a rod placed in his femur today, and woke up and looked at me when I made rounds tonight. He responds to his father's voice; just goes to show once again that it pays to be 18 years old.

All patients continue in great spirits. It is delightful to watch them. We had wheelchair races between patients on the deck today, much to their delight. Our little 4 year old who had severe burn contractures of his knees was one of the participants, and I got to watch him laugh out loud for the first time.

Engineering went ashore today, but note that they are running out of things to do there. They still have a few motors to rework, and hope to take some work teams in to help the Germans place some lavatories and deliver water jerry cans to IDP camps over the next couple of weeks. The Spanish are building a new helo pad at the hospital starting tomorrow.

We are still seeking information about a possible assist visit to Meleuboh.

Communications are poor between here and Meleuboh, and we are awaiting word from the embassy about whether security concerns might prevent a trip there.

We are sending a sizable team ashore tomorrow, 40+ people. In addition, we will have some Germans come back to the ship tomorrow night, as well as 7 surgeons from Abidin Hospital who want to confer with our surgeons and visit the ship. We are working with them to enable our exit strategy from Banda Aceh.

Finally, a stickball game was held on the flight deck for all hands tonight as the sun went down. It ended when the ball disappeared into the Indian Ocean. We have duct tape; another will be ready for tomorrow night's game.

Bill McDaniel

I have mentioned security concerns several times. Certainly there were major problems in Sumatra prior to the tsunami, and a civil war had been the status quo for many years between the GAM (rebels) and TNI (government troops). However, the head of the TNI assured me early on that the GAM had let them know there would be no hostilities for the indefinite future as long as the country was recovering from the tsunami. That status remained; there had been no hostilities during the time we had been there. However, the host nation and our government were acutely aware that hostilities could resume at any time. Therefore, ultimately we were denied a continued presence in Meleuboh; just too far removed from the majority of our assets. And, while they certainly could have benefited from our being there, the folks of Banda Aceh were delighted that we did not move; after all, they managed to keep us gainfully employed!

Subject: 26 Feb 2005 report to my friends

"helo dr.johnson, I am from Aceh, and my close friend is your patient at Mercy, his name is AMRI. do you remember? his got accident with the truck, I think you remember him. my name is dian, amri asked me to send you to tell you that he going to be better now, thank you for the sucsessfull operation in Mercy. and as the acheness I really want to say Thank you very much for everythings that you and your country done to my peoples. Thank you very much. and I will always report to you about amri's condition. and I am so sorry coz my english not very well see yaa docter......"

Perhaps this does not need any amplification. It is an email one of our oral surgeons received yesterday. It represents what I have said all along. A dignified, thankful, resilient, humble, and proud people, these Acehinese. Or, as Dian says, 'acheness.'

Ache..ness."

There is a message in that misspelling.

I don't really remember which patients I have talked about. We continue to be busy, most of us continue to cry occasionally, and they continue on in their dignity.

Our little 14 year old sweetheart whose arm we had to amputate because of bone cancer went home yesterday. She had a 7 hour car ride to get through, followed by a 2 hour moped ride to get home. She will die within a year or so; nothing we can do about it. The best minds Harvard has to offer have looked at her case and concluded that chemotherapy would just make her miserable, and not cure her. She has smiled and laughed continually since we admitted her 3 weeks ago. We have a most wonderful room set up in the children's ward, where the kids...and their parents...draw. We tape the results up, and I have carefully catalogued them. When I am able, I will send the results out as a photo album. Little comment will be needed. Happy, sad, death, hope, thanks. Readily recognizable in the drawings. Our fourteen year old has done the majority of the drawings. She is a talented artist. She left like she lived each day. A little smile, a wave, and as her English has rapidly improved, a "Thank you." We will never see her again. Nor will we ever forget her. Iqbal, our eleven year old I have talked about before. He lost all of his family in the tsunami, and was himself pulled from the sea 2 km from shore many hours later, clinging to a piece of driftwood. He came to us as a tiny, wasted little boy in respiratory arrest. We intubated him and had him on a ventilator. The doctors performed their wizardry, and the nurses gave their care and love, and Iqbal got well. He was extubated, and started eating like there was no tomorrow. Maybe he is well aware that that is a real possibility, I don't know. He ate six meals a day, donned sunglasses and was wheeled up on deck, then started slow faltering steps. Within ten days of getting off the respirator he had gained 10 pounds and had laid claim to everyone's affection. He donned his protective helmet for the first helo ride he remembers, and left us yesterday with his uncle. He strode happily to the helo, looked back, waved, and got on with his life. If anyone deserves to live out of this horrific mess, it is Iqbal. We have had successes, and we have had patients we could do nothing for. Even our failures shake our hands, dip their heads, touch their right hand to their hearts, and thank us. They all love to have their pictures taken, and we all stay busy taking digital pictures and rapidly depleting the stores of the ship's supply of colored printing ink. We get the pictures blown up, and they are taped up beside the beds until they leave, when they are proudly and carefully taken away by the patients. And, they don't like having their pictures taken by themselves. They always want their friends, and their doctors, and their nurses in the pictures with them. They like people, and definitely find strength in each other, and in us. I could write more stories about each of these remarkable people. Each story would make you cry, if you allowed it, and few would make you laugh. However, the people themselves would make you laugh from their sheer joy. No matter their story, they love to smile and laugh. All you have to do is smile and wave, even when walking down the streets of Banda Aceh, and suddenly all the faces light up with smiles of their own. They wave, and the girls giggle, and the little boys all want to pose, as all little boys are wont to do everywhere.

I went to Meleuboh, about 100 miles south of here, on Monday. Again, the story is the same. Meleuboh is only a few miles from the epicenter of the 9.0 earthquake of 26 DEC 2004. Everyone felt the earthquake, then ran out to see if each other was all right. The water crest hit Meleuboh within minutes of the quake. I don't know the real height or speed of the wave, but it is reported at about 70 feet, and traveling somewhere in excess of 100 miles per hour. Regardless, everyone within one-half mile or so of the waterfront died instantly. Now, the WHO and UN have set up a IDP (internally displaced persons) camp in the middle of the town, and in front of each tent families sit. Not sad. They all laugh and wave. Many ask, "USA?" I always give a thumbs up and get the same in return, and sometimes a hug. Off at the edge of the camp is a large blue tent. "Children's Center." I went in, and there were 50 children of all ages who were playing. All orphans, or who lost at least one parent in the tsunami and earthquake. No sad faces. Laughing, posing, bouncing, playing. A beautiful little 10 year old girl came up with her 8 month old brother in her arms. Little fat kid. Looked sort of like me at that age, or maybe now. He reached out his arms and I happily held him for the next 10 or 15 minutes. He was content. So was I. I realize that these letters are repetitive to a degree. How many ways can you say that you love a people? How many ways can you say how good and dignified and proud a people can be? I don't have that many ways in me, so I can only repeat it. But, every time I say it I mean it at least as much as the last time. You should too.

I will leave here on Mercy in mid-March, and should be home shortly thereafter.

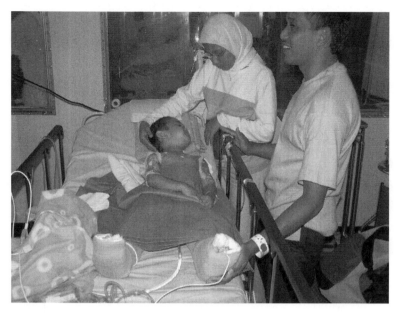

Zahrul following burn scar removal and leg straightening

Chapter 9

Subject: Sitrep Banda Aceh 5 March

THREE DAYS AGO our OB/GYN surgeons operated upon a 21 year old woman. She had lost her entire family in the tsunami, and was referred to us for a tumor in her abdomen. A basketball sized 7.5 pound tumor was removed on Wednesday, and it did not appear to be a typical ovarian cyst. Tonight as everyone settled down for a serious evening of Bingo, the pathologist brought the path report into the OB doctor, who suddenly jumped up in obvious glee. The tumor was a teratoma, a benign tumor, and one that means this young lady's string of bad luck might have ceased. We hope. She's doing super!

Otherwise my day consisted mostly of sitting down in the playroom on Ward 1, watching the kids, their parents, and the staff...well, play. I've never seen such a happy hospital ward. I just relaxed and enjoyed it, snapping occasional pictures of the delightful scene, then going to get them printed so that the kids could have them; they love their pictures, as I have noted before.

We bid good bye to two of our favorites today, our 4 year old boy with a hare lip repair, and our 4 year old burn victim. The little hare lip repair child was a perfect picture in his cranial (helmet) and a shy smile as he waved good bye. The burn victim came in a month ago as a scared, scarred little boy who was unable to walk. He left jumping up and down in excitement about getting on the helicopter and laughing. Again, not a bad send off.

Our 8 month old is holding her own; she may be a candidate for a very prolonged hospitalization, and with that she should live. With the professional physician and nursing staff she has concentrating on her, they won't let her slip away, we hope. (This was an infant that had inexplicably been operated upon in a local hospital for "appendicitis." She was septic when we acquired her.)

CDR Kurt Hummeldorf, the oral surgeon, again made a major difference in a 27 year old woman's life. She came in with a benign tumor of her jaw about the size of a cantaloupe, hanging down the left side of her face onto her chest. She was embarrassed and did not want anyone to see her. Kurt and his associates removed the tumor and the lower jaw bone on that side in an 8 hour surgery, with one of the Project Hope orthopedic surgeons removing bone from her pelvis to help replace the jawbone...along with a rib the woman wasn't using all that much. Amazing surgery, again!

1. We saw 253 patients on shore today, admitted 3 plus 3 escorts, and discharged 8. The optometry clinic still reigns supreme, passing out 192 pairs of glasses. We discovered today that the local radio station is advertising our 'free glasses' service 4 times a day on the air; having given away several thousand pairs of glasses thus far, we rightly assumed someone had figured it out. The eye team had an abbreviated day today, moving their equipment into a new location that should provide a little better crowd control.

2. We have two German physicians aboard, plus two TNI dentists who will be with us for a few days working with our folks.

3. Our nurses again were the principal educators at Abidin nursing school today for 25 nursing students. Next week we will offer Basic Life Support (BLS) classes for all the Emergency Room physicians and nursing staff at Abidin.

4. Medical repair continues to fix everything in sight: a surgical microscope, an infusion pump, 2 nebulizers, and they are working to bring all the new equipment at Abidin into use. They have had the folks there gather all the new and old equipment in one large room, and the techs will work next week at making everything usable. The engineers installed a new motor in the sewage treatment plant, and continued to work on fixing up the tool shop at Abidin.

5. CAPT McFarland had a meeting with the midwives at Abidin, working with them, and will do so again next week.

6. 31 patients were seen at TNI hospital by our team there, part of the above total count. Plus, our Project Hope surgeon assisted and helped modify the technique of the TNI surgeon on 4 hernia repairs there.

-Our Project Hope anesthesiologist checked out all the OR equipment, supplies, etc, and concluded that we can do simple surgeries there. However, their instruments are extremely limited, and are quite old. We should have some excess that might be of value to them, and will take our own equipment in next week when we do surgery there with them.

-Several cases are coming up next week in general surgery and ortho that our surgeons will assist them with.

-If possible we will bring 13 cataract patients out next week to Mercy for surgery.

7. CDR Murphy is working with IOM to help with infection control at multiple IDP camps in the area.

8. The Australians had been spraying the grounds at Abidin for mosquitoes; now that they are gone the problem is getting bad again. We will request the EPMU team to come over and help out.

9. Our psychiatrists continue to work aggressively every day with UNICEF. Again, though we say little about these outreach programs, they are extremely valuable and have a significant positive effect for the future.

10. Everyone is being directed to start writing down their successful Standard Operating Procedures so that we can gather them as 'lessons learned' for future actions like this...assuming that there is ever something like this again.

We continue to work hard, and to achieve more than anyone here dared hope we would. We can certainly do better; there is nothing that can't be improved on. For a first time effort, however, not bad at all. And, the partnership between Project Hope, the Public Health Service, the civilian staff operating the ship, and the Navy could not be better. This concept is a winner, and we need to develop it for the future.

Bill McDaniel

It was about this time that we got an interesting message from Senator Bill Frist's office in DC. Senator Frist was then the Majority Leader of the Senate. A team of engineers from Tennessee had come to Indonesia to assist in evaluating the water supply and cleaning and rebuilding water wells. While there one of them started having stomach pains. As the pain became more severe he and a friend traveled to Banda Aceh to see if they could find a doctor who might examine him. Knowing nothing of Mercy's presence, they walked into Abidin Hospital for an evaluation. The first thing they noted was that it looked like the hospital had been destroyed! Well, they were at least observant. Then they saw a cat run out of the operating room. They looked at each other and decided that in spite of the stomach pain, they might try to find a more suitable medical care facility!

They had noted the large white ship with large red crosses circling off the coast, and correctly assumed it was medical. Not knowing of the presence of American doctors at Abidin Hospital, they got on their satellite phone and called their Senator's office, inquiring if he knew anything about that hospital ship. He did.

So, we sent a helo to Banda Aceh and retrieved the two gentlemen, and our surgeons removed the offending appendix from the one with the belly pain. They spent several days aboard Mercy and seemed to greatly enjoy and appreciate the experience. They were especially appreciative that we kept cats out of our operating rooms.

Subject: Sitrep Banda Aceh 4 March.

Our latest long term patient departing tomorrow is Zharul, the four year old who came in a month ago with severe burn contractures of his knees. He had not walked in 2 years. Our burn surgeons straightened his knees out to full extension in one surgery, then took him back later and skin grafted the areas behind his knees. It has been painful watching this young non-smiling boy struggle, not really crying much, when we all knew he was in such pain. Well, the last few days he has delighted at grabbing a wheelchair or an EKG machine on wheels and chasing nurses and corpsmen around the ward. He has rhythm! He stands and dances to the music now, knees straight. We have made a difference in his life, believe me. He leaves tomorrow. By the way, he finally is smiling a lot.

We have a 57 year old woman here who has diabetes and severe electrolyte disturbances. She lost her niece in the tsunami, and her husband a week later to a stroke. She gave up, and her family brought her in when they could no longer get her to respond. Our folks have stabilized her, and our psychiatrists and chaplain have helped her turn the corner. I think she will be able to live a while longer, perhaps with a little more peace in her life.

Our little 8 month old baby with the perforated bowel still is hanging on. One of the Project Hope doctors, Dr. Braner, a pediatric intensive specialist, virtually lives at her bedside, and has been there since he was called out after one hour of orientation on the 24th of February. She still has a long way to go, but he and many other professionals are desperately trying to make a difference in her life as well.

We have the tragic ones; a seventeen month old delightful boy with a liver tumor, a hepato-blastoma. Massive. Surgery alone will just kill him; he needs chemotherapy to precede the surgery. We are exploring options there.

1. Another busy day today. 4 major surgeries, 3 operating room angiograms. 333 patients total seen on shore between TNI and Abidin Hospitals. 244 pairs of glasses prescribed among those. two discharges, five patients admitted, including three pediatric hernias who traveled five hours to be seen here.

2. CDR Clark worked at Abidin Nursing School again, teaching. Next week a team will do BLS (Basic Life Support) certification for the OR, ER, and ICU nurses there. One fact of interest about Abidin; as has been noted before, many of their staff are missing. They have no nursing support in the hospital at night; families provide any care needed, and if they do it as well as they help aboard ship, they are doing a super job.

3. Medical repair continues to help rebuild things, repairing 2 anesthesia machines today, plus one ultra sound machine. There is a new ultra sound machine coming in, and they will calibrate it and train the Abidin staff on its use. The engineers as well continue their super work, taking in 500 feet of cable today, and 10 gallons of paint with which they painted the tool shop at Abidin...which they had pressure washed yesterday. They installed a motor, and are working on the oxygen system, which has multiple leaks. Someone has donated an oxygen and nitrous oxide making machine, which will be installed soon. The five local engineers who have been hired started working today.

4. At TNI (military hospital) we had 5 physicians and two nurses today. They saw a total of 55 patients. One of our corpsmen gave a course on the proper use of a spine board. They sent one patient to Mercy for a head CT scan, who was then returned to TNI. The TNI and our physicians paired off together and made rounds together for a good part of the day. Lots of pathology was found,

and we hope to start using their operating rooms to do surgery, leaving the patients there for follow on care. That possibility will be explored tomorrow.

5. Our UNICEF team continues their collaborative relationship there, and another 5 days of interactive infrastructure building will be done this next week.

6. We had five doctors and nurses from ICRC (International Red Cross Hospital) hospital and two from the German tent hospital aboard today working with our folks here. We continue to be extremely busy, and some amazingly large surgical cases continue to be done aboard Mercy. We are working hard at trying to accomplish a smooth exit strategy, hoping to have minimal impact of a sudden nature in Banda Aceh. However, the truth is that Abidin will not be fully up to speed for 6 months to a year, and the many capabilities of Mercy will be sorely missed. Everyone ashore is aware that we have to leave, and is appreciative of the efforts our folks are making to help them as much as possible before that time.

One last note. I talked at length with a Los Angeles Times reporter last night about what he has seen here. He reported that he went out with teams gathering up dead bodies yesterday. After two months the bodies are badly decomposed, but the adults almost all had cell phones in their pockets when they died. The search teams remove the SIM cards from the found phones, slip them into one of theirs, and dial the last number called. They found two families yesterday who had lost all hope of ever finding the bodies of their loved ones. While this does not give them a daughter or a son back, it does allow them the dignity of a formal burial, and allows them closure.

Bill McDaniel

I realize that there is repetition in this narrative. However, with daily sitreps and my occasional mass emailing as the basis of this tale, I will repeat frequently. On the other hand, as you are reading this you probably get somewhat confused about the specific details of the various patients, so maybe this will be of some positive value! (Or, add to the confusion?) Below is the email I sent out on 6 March to my list. As I have mentioned, the Indonesian government had established an end point for the mass world response. March 26. They felt that they should be able to assume the burden by that time. Maybe. We were working toward departing on 19 March, with Mercy having spent 6.5 weeks on station.

6 March 2005

I sit here feeling very frustrated. There is little I can say that I have not said before.

The people continue to be as delightful as ever. We continue to do big surgeries that are life changing to those we work on, and continue to see people beyond our capabilities to repair...or anyone's...and we have to send them back home to die soon. We have seen some of the most horrific end stage cancer patients you can imagine...and we are usually the first medical folks they have ever consulted, unfortunately. I sat tonight with our head and neck surgeons and reviewed CT scans; simply some of the most amazing examples of pathology ever put together. That's not good news, by the way. It's not good in medicine to be called the most amazing of almost anything, except for those several "most amazing cures" here we have been privileged to be a part of.

We have many exceptions to bad news, of course. I have written about some of them. Three days ago our OB/GYN surgeons operated upon a 21 year old woman. She had lost her entire family in the tsunami, and was referred to us for a tumor in her abdomen. A basketball sized 7.5 pound tumor was removed on Wednesday, and it did not appear to be a typical ovarian cyst. Tonight as everyone settled down for a serious evening of Bingo, (We are on a ship, after all, and entertainment is minimal!) the pathologist brought the path report into the OB doctor, who suddenly jumped up in obvious glee. The tumor was a teratoma, a benign tumor, and one that means this

114

young lady's string of bad luck might have ceased. We hope. She's doing super!

My day today consisted mostly of sitting down in the playroom filled with patient drawings on Ward 1, watching the kids, their parents, and the staff...well, play. I've never seen such a happy hospital ward. I just relaxed and enjoyed it, snapping occasional pictures of the delightful scene, then going to get them printed so that the kids could have them; they love their pictures, as I have noted before.

We bid good bye to two of our favorites today, our 4 year old boy with a hare lip repair, and our 4 year old burn victim. The little hare lip repair child was a perfect picture in his cranial protection and a shy smile as he waved good bye as he tentatively walked to the helicopter.

The burn victim came in a month ago as a scared, scarred little boy who had been unable to walk for two years and who was unwilling to smile, perhaps because there was nothing to smile about in his life. After several surgeries he has straight legs, and has suddenly learned how much fun it is to chase people with an EKG machine on wheels as his battering ram! He left jumping up and down in excitement about getting on the helicopter, laughing gleefully all the while. Again, not a bad send off. These young men won't remember us too long, though I expect that helicopter ride will be in their memories forever. Meanwhile, they will remain in our memories....forever.

Our oral surgeons again made a major difference in a twenty-seven year old woman's life. She came in with a benign tumor of her jaw about the size of a cantaloupe, hanging down the left side of her face onto her chest. She was embarrassed and did not want anyone to see her. They removed the tumor and the lower jaw bone on that side in an eight hour surgery, with one of the Project Hope orthopedic surgeons removing bone from her pelvis to help replace the jawbone...along with a rib the woman wasn't using all that much. Amazing surgery, again!

We have a seventeen month old beautiful little boy who has a major liver tumor, who may well not live much longer. We have an equally beautiful little nine year old girl (who looks 4) with only minimal kidney function left. She is happy and playful, but needs a kidney to remain that way. We are exploring getting one for her. We have.....so many of these. So many beautiful children. So many hopeful adults. So many successes...and so many we cannot help. If we were truly as good as they all think or hope we were, we could save them all. No one is that good. I wish we were.

We are soon to leave here. We are slowly finding institutions to ship our most serious patients out to, while hoping we can still cure all of them before we have to do that. Our teams ashore are working frantically trying, ever trying, to teach and help and build and continue the quest to leave them measurably better for our presence here. I think we will accomplish that goal, but there is always so much more to be done for these wonderful people, these Acehinese. We are doing surgery ashore in both the Abidin University and the TNI military hospitals, assisting their surgeons, having them assist us, leaving behind equipment to make their job a little easier, and always sharing everything of ourselves that we can. That's all we can do. Is it enough? None of us thinks so, really, but....that's all we can do.

I will write one more of these in 10 days and let you all know how those days went. That one will be hard to write, I fear, as we look back over the railings of the ship and watch this ruined city, this rebuilding city, these vibrant people, recede into the distance.

Bill McDaniel

We were all frustrated. We were all happy with what we had accomplished, but all fully realized that much, much more could be done. While we cannot always save the world, all those out there as responders really want to do that. We realized fully that we had an incredible medical platform to work off of in USNS Mercy, but also realized that we were only utilizing perhaps 15% of her capabilities.

Why not bring more? Mostly politics, I fear. We certainly had enough volunteer medical personnel around the country to fully staff the ship, and thus vastly increase our throughput and capabilities.

We were limited by several things. First, political will. A number of people in the government would have preferred that we not be doing this mission at all. And, if we were to do it, we should be limited markedly in what we offered. While that was disturbing to most of us, in fairness I must also note that if we had been fully staffed we would have a tremendous problem with logistics. Getting patients and escorts to and from the ship was not an easy task and really had to be done with helicopters. There was no pier space available to dock at. Security was always a concern, even though there had been no credible threat while we were there. Still, always a concern. We had three helicopters dedicated to the mission. If we were running at full capacity a fleet of helos would have been required. We just did not have them.

So, all in all we lived with our frustrations and did all we could. Knowing all the while that we could have done much, much more, and would have been able to save many more lives and limbs.

You just can't do everything. But, you don't have to like it.

I mentioned earlier in this treatise that on occasion we had admitted a forty-one year old man from the German hospital. He had necrotizing pancreatitis and had received 3 surgeries; he was septic and beyond their capabilities to help any more. We had the head of infectious disease from Mass General and other specialists, so brought him and his wife aboard to try our hand at a cure.

The specialists, nurses, corpsmen, and social workers worked with him day and night, taking him to surgery in the middle of the night trying to effect a cure. Finally, after tremendous effort, all decided that he was beyond our help. His wife was informed that he would die soon, and she responded (through the interpreter, always), asking if we could return them to Indonesian soil so he could die there. Clearly we could do so. He was transferred to a gurney for his trip to the flight deck, but as his gurney was wheeled from the ICU, his wife stopped it. She asked that all those who had been working with her husband please gather around. A sizable number of personnel, all upset at being unable to save this gentle man, did so. Through the interpreter she made a simple, but oh-so-eloquent speech.

"I know you all wanted my husband to live, as did we. However, ultimately you must realize that it is not our will that matters; it is God's will. And, God has chosen otherwise. We want you all to understand that these last 5 days have been the happiest of our lives. You have taken us into your family, have given us wonderful medical care and your love, and now give us the ultimate dignity of allowing my husband to die on his home soil. So, please do not be sad. God has chosen his course. It is not our choice that matters. Thank you so very much."

And they left to the helo and home, where he died shortly thereafter.

I wandered into the ICU shortly after he had left, and was startled to find everyone with their heads down, crying. They told me the above story.

I called my wife that night. Now, in thirty-five years of marriage she had never seen me cry. As I related the events of the day, and went into this story, I suddenly started crying so hard that I laid the phone down for a few minutes as I sobbed. Remember when you were a kid and cried over something so hard you thought you might die…and it would serve them right it you did!? Well, that's how I cried. When I finally picked the phone up again my wife asked me if I was going to be okay.

Yep, I am and I was, but that was the nature of these incredible people we were being privileged to help.

Young patients waiting to leave the ship with their mothers

Chapter 10

Subject: Sitrep Banda Aceh 7 March

WE ARE SLOWLY winding down, and the patients are lining up in longer numbers. Our screeners came in today with 25 patients who need...and want...surgery. We can't do all of them, but will certainly do some that we can get in and out quickly. I certainly don't blame the patients for trying to get in; I would as well if I were them.

Sad news today. We had a little girl in late February with tubercular meningitis who we transferred to Jakarta; we just did not have the ability to care for her many problems long term. She died there a few days later. Not due to bad medicine on their part, just a very ill little girl.

119

Our little 8 month old girl with the perforated bowel is hanging on, but as I watched her a few minutes ago she is having increasing difficulty breathing. A chest X-ray is being done now. Her malnourished body cannot take much more of an insult and survive. All we can do is keep practicing good medicine and pray.

Everyone else is doing OK. Some major recuperating being done down on the wards at the moment, but they should all be off Mercy by 14 March.

1. 253 patients seen ashore today between Abidin and TNI Hospitals. As usual, optometry wins the prize with 169 pairs of glasses dispensed. 5 patients and 5 escorts home, and 3 plus 3 admitted. 4 surgeries done yesterday (a no fly day), and 5 surgeries done today. We continue to do lots of surgery, and lots of major cases.

2. Our nurse educators continue to shine, working with the 60 nursing students at Abidin today. They will start BLS (basic life support) training tomorrow, and will continue all week, with 25-30 doctors and nurses in each day's classes.

3. Engineering rebuilt and installed an air compressor today at Abidin, and installed 15 oxygen bottles into their system. The standby diesel generator at Abidin will not start; we have a battery that will work in it, and it will be installed tomorrow.

4. The Chaplain is working with engineering on a project. Engineering is buying some pipe for flow of sewage and ground water for a section of the hospital system that has been crushed. The Chaplain is taking a crew of ten volunteers and they will spend 3 days laying the pipe, returning to Mercy to be hosed down on the flight deck before being allowed inside the ship afterward. The 2 or 3 days following that the Chaplain will take a volunteer crew to the various children's camps, along with UNICEF, for distribution of toys.

5. At TNI today, we instructed 13 nurses on proper care of burn patients. A total of 64 patients were seen there, part of the total number noted above. We took several large bags of supplies into the hospital.

-One of our Project Hope orthopedic surgeons operated at TNI with the Indonesian orthopedic surgeon. She said his skills were good; they had to be, inasmuch as the lights went out 3 times in the OR. They keep flashlights handy, and no one seems to miss a beat in surgery. Luckily, the patients are asleep and unaware of this.

-The Project Hope OB doctor saw quite a few patients there as well. For the sake of those non-medical folks who read this, I will not go into detail about some of her cases. She did, however!

-The anesthesia support at TNI is from 2 CRNA (nurse anesthetists). They are quite good, but are very short on equipment. We will help them out where possible.

6. The UNICEF team continued their work with 35 people at the psych hospital. A point to ponder: The psych hospital had 220 staff before the tsunami. They have 40 now.

-They have requested that our Moslem Chaplain come in tomorrow to assist.

7. EPMU (preventive medicine unit) came to the hospital today upon request and sprayed for mosquitoes heavily. They will continue to do so in the coming days.

8. The Project Hope vet went ashore today, and reported that the state of the veterinary community is just as bad as the medical community was right after the tsunami, but they have had no subsequent help. They need virtually everything, and he notes that it will take a major effort to repair their infrastructure.

9. I had out-briefs with the heads of the UNICEF and WHO missions here today. Very positive overall. A few pertinent points were:

-Both stressed that by not being able to be ashore at night during our time here we missed lots of opportunities to interact and plan. Both stressed that if we do this again they will be happy to allow shore parties to stay at their compounds and be protected by their security.

-Both were extremely complimentary of the US military effort here. UNICEF stated that "We could not have survived without it."

-The WHO head told me that 2 years ago DOD sponsored a workshop with all the UN agencies and others on 'the role of the military in humanitarian assist mission.' She said the antipathy was such that at the end of the workshop the conclusion was that the military should do their own thing; there was no combined role possible. However, today **she noted that we need to have this workshop again, inasmuch as the civil-military team here has been so highly successful. We must capture the lessons learned to plan for future joint missions!** A remarkable turnaround. She asked me to pass this up the chain of command and urge that such a workshop take place as soon as practical.

-UNICEF is extremely happy with the psychosocial and child protection teams' integration with them. Again, they asked me if it might be possible for these teams to continue working with them for the next 3 months. She said that while they can always find bodies to do the work, it is the philosophy of our folks that is so in line with theirs. She specifically mentioned Dr. John Perez as having the perfect approach for them. I told her that I would pass this along to RDML Craig Vanderwagen so he could talk to his bosses about the request.

-The head of WHO strongly requested that DOD again provide a liaison to work with them on a full time basis. She said there was one at one time, but no longer. She is so delighted at the WHO-military cooperation here now that she wants to continue to build on it.

Bill McDaniel

This sitrep was a key one. In my out-briefs with UNICEF and WHO, both parties stressed repeatedly the value of the incredible cooperation between our military and their organizations, and the fact that we had been able to accomplish so much. They desperately wanted this cooperation to continue. Unfortunately it has not.

Why not? I'm not sure. Probably the biggest reason is that there was no champion of close cooperation in our senior military medical leadership…especially the civilian leadership of the military medical system. Why not? Again, I have no idea. Did they just think the idea had no real merit? Perhaps. I think that it just was not something on their radar screen. In the various major disasters we have faced worldwide since 2005, I have remained in close contact with the senior WHO personnel. They continue to do incredible work, and our military response continues to achieve phenomenal results. Just not in concert. We go in and do our thing…and an amazing thing it is…and get out. They do the same, though on a much longer term basis. But, could we do far better? Absolutely! For whatever reason we just don't make the cooperative effort as much as we could.

Would it require a major effort on our part? No, actually it would not. Our maritime services (Navy, Marines, Coast Guard) recognized the value of our medical response in Indonesia and in a new "At Sea" doctrine published in 2007 firmly established our medical response in Disaster Relief and Humanitarian Response situations as an essential part of our doctrine. We do this now with both hospital ships and with ships of the line, in Asia, Africa, and Latin America. We do tremendous good in these efforts, working in close concert with many civilian organizations like Project Hope.

Thus we have already stepped out smartly in response; we just need to go the little extra mile. There are many retired senior military medical officers who would be ideal to work as liaison officers between WHO, the NGO's, and the US military, completing a link that is desperately needed. And, we don't need a lot of personnel to do this. Two or three would be adequate, with them having the ability to call on other personnel when disasters pile up. The expense would be minimal, the results incalculably good.

There is one problem, however. The person selected for this task would need access to the most senior US military person running the operation. Not only access but trust. And, that person would have to be in a position to do something that the military really, really does not like. Violate the Chain of Command. The person in this position should be on the ground in the disaster

123

response scenario and be able to contact the senior person immediately when a decision was made at some point in the Chain of Command that violated common sense. Not that the retired person would have permission to counteract the order, just allowed to have access to argue the case. Because, and you can trust me on this, when there are multiple staffs involved in oversight in these situations…and most of them thousands of miles away…invariably there are some dumb decisions made…with the best of intent always. Someone needs to have enough experience and oversight to recognize these poor decisions and have the access to at least argue the point.

Frankly, I doubt that we will ever get there. We will continue to do wonderful work in disaster relief, but it is always frustrating knowing it could be so much better if we just worked in loose concert with the other agencies in the field.

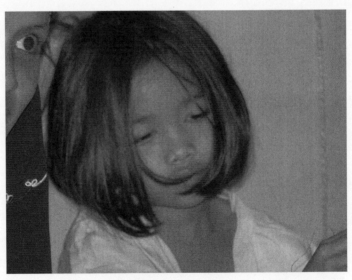

Tara, a beautiful young girl with a foot deformity

Subject: sitrep Banda Aceh 8 March

Our little eight month old girl (post appendectomy) is not doing well. Her doctors talked with the mother at length, and if there is no improvement over night, she wants to have the baby transported back to Abidin University Hospital tomorrow afternoon and the breathing tube removed. Our folks have remained at the baby's bedside constantly for 2 weeks now, but it is not looking good. I sat in the ICU for a while this evening watching the mother stroke the baby's head as she read her Koran.

The ICU is a busy place, and resembles a major teaching hospital. There were 7 patients there tonight, either very ill or post surgery from very major procedures. About 15 doctors were gathered discussing each patient; I listened for a while, and realized that as a seldom practicing orthopedic surgeon I had nothing to contribute! They are all intelligent, involved, and very, very knowledgeable. Again, one of the many benefits of this civil-military partnership.

1. A busy day today. We discharged five patients and their escorts, and admitted 7 more with their escorts. A total of 559 patients were seen between TNI and Abidin Hospitals, 415 of them being seen by optometry. At this point Optometry has passed out about 4,100 pairs of glasses, 1000 pairs of which have been ground at night by our opticians aboard Mercy. And amazing output. We have only 900 pairs of glasses left, and will be out of glasses by no later than Friday. We did 9 surgeries on Mercy, and our surgeons did several more at TNI hospital with their Indonesian colleagues. 2 Indonesian pharmacists came to Mercy today for a visit.

2. Our nursing instructors at Abidin continue to further the medical knowledge of the folks there. They taught their first BLS course today, and the 17 nurses who completed it were clearly thrilled when they received their certificates.

3. Our lab officer went to both Abidin and TNI today, working with 3 techs and the pathologist on materials new to them.

4. The engineers continued their forcible assault on the machines at Abidin, fixing and installing a water pump. They purchased 25 feet of cement drain line for tomorrow's pipeline laying venture. The electricians are working on backup power for TNI hospital.

5. As we continue our drawdown (I realize 9 surgeries do not sound like much of a drawdown, but it is happening.) in surgery aboard Mercy, TNI, ICRC, and Abidin have expressed interest in our surgeons coming to those places to help with cases. We will still have to be very selective with case selection, however. Unfortunately, the people in the surrounding hills and villages are just now starting to show up en mass to take advantage of our presence. They repeatedly tell our folks that they 'love Americans.' Even when we tell them that we cannot do surgery because we are leaving, they still thank us and politely leave with smiles in place. It is difficult for everyone.

6. At TNI hospital 148 patients were seen. 9 nurses were taught how to do triage. OB helped deliver a baby today who had aspiration pneumonia. They placed a chest tube and intubated the baby and transferred it to Abidin. Our OB doctors will operate at TNI on Thursday.

-In addition, as we draw down surgery, our pediatric physicians are increasing their presence in evaluating many children in out-patient clinics at TNI, and 2 pediatricians will work there tomorrow and probably the rest of the week.

-The PH (Project Hope) surgeon did 2 cases at Abidin today.

7. The UNICEF psych team continues to work daily, and will do so until Saturday.

The team that went to ICRC hospital today reported that Elisa, our tsunami lung and brain abscess little girl who has been paralyzed on the left side, came out and waved at them today...with her left hand. She was walking for the first time today as well.

Finally, I talked with one of our PH emergency room physicians today when she came back from working all day in the ER at TNI hospital. She is usually of constant good cheer and always has a smile. Almost. She was exhausted.

"It's hard in there. A constant stream of patients, many very ill that we can do little for. Just before I left a man came in with a sub-arachnoid (brain) bleed. He'll die there. There is nothing we can do for him."

This inability to meet the tremendous need here is physically and emotionally exhausting. The infrastructure will not be adequate to address that need for a long, long time. Meanwhile, however, our folks are giving all they can give toward that goal.

Bill McDaniel

There is not a lot to add to this at this point. We continue to go ashore daily, and while it seems that we have been here forever, there is so much that we have been unable to accomplish. Yep, we know that we have done a lot for many people; but, truly, we could stay here for years and stay just as busy.

Subject: Sitrep Banda Aceh 9 March

Ah, well. Our little 8 month old patient who came to us toxic following a surgical problem ashore died today. She died at Abidin Hospital, about 30 minutes after she and her mother were taken back. The 3 Pediatric ICU nurses and the pediatric intensive care doctor who have been watching and caring for her and Mom since 25 February all went in with her and were there when she died. The little thing just could not get past chronic malnourishment and bad infections. Her mother has been reading the Koran and singing quietly for the last 36 hours. The nurses prepared a beautiful memory package of pictures and mementos for Mom, and the staff took up a collection to get her home, several hours out of Banda Aceh. We fully realize we can't win them all...but we sure would have liked to have won this one.

We did have other good outcomes today. Our 5 year old girl who came in with what was thought to be a big spleen had a large diseased kidney removed today, and looks like she will do well post op. We took the metal fixation hardware out of the back of a 35 year old 'strong spirited' (her husband's phrase) woman's back a few days ago. She has been paraplegic for years, but is quite a force at home, so her fisherman husband says. She is delightful, and our orthopedic surgeons did her a major favor by removing infected hardware from her back.

Tara, a beautiful 8 year old girl with a foot tumor (Elves' foot) had a below knee amputation 2 days ago. Tonight she was laughing and playing. Handicap International is on the ground in BA, and already has her scheduled for a prosthesis fitting.

We had a new, honorary physician in surgery today; more on him later.

1. We saw a total of 400 patients today, 277 of them eye patients. Most were seen at TNI military hospital. There were 8 discharges and 3 admissions, one of which is a little 2 year old with a large spleen (most likely thalasemia) and a very low blood count. Removal of the spleen will give this kid a normal life, so CDR McDonald again showed her fine initiative in bringing the child out for surgery...in spite of an 'official' cessation of new cases to be admitted. A good call on her part, but she makes them routinely, so that's no surprise. 6 surgeries were done today.

2. Our hard working engineers finished painting the workshop at Abidin, and found another air compressor to overhaul. Lars (one of our civilian engineers) then went to TNI and had to suit up for surgery, working on the emergency backup lighting in the OR as a case was going on. He successfully installed backup battery powered lights, and the surgeons were delighted at his success. I promise you that if the patients were aware, they would be delighted as well.

-Lars reported that a new team of Australian engineers have arrived, and will relieve the Germans and Americans who have been maintaining the place for the last 6 weeks. He notes that they are highly qualified.

3. At ICRC our medical technicians worked on their ultra sound machine, fixing it, and are working on their sterilizer. We will give them 4 oxygen bottles and couplings to use in their out-patient department. ICRC is being superbly cooperative in promising to take virtually any patient we have in order to allow us to leave on time. We have taken about 35 of their patients for surgery in the last 6 weeks.

4. CDR Clark and her team of instructors worked with 72 nursing students at Abidin today, as well as 20 other nurses and doctors earning their BLS certificates from them. Tomorrow the same numbers will be helped.

5. The UNICEF/psych teaching coordination in a 5 day program completed its 2nd day today, very successfully.

6. At TNI Hospital our folks worked with 13 nursing students on basic sterilization and cleanliness techniques with babies and their supplies.

-2 Mexican ships showed up today, and some of their surgeons came to TNI and interacted with our surgeons. They hope to step in and start assisting when we leave.

-Last week one of our technicians worked with the nurses at TNI and taught them how to intubate patients. Last night 2 TNI soldiers were brought in with heat exhaustion (another had already died), and one of the nurses who had been in the class managed to successfully intubate both of them, saving their lives. She was quite proud when she was showing her patients off today, as she had a right to be. Again, these people are quick learners, and our actions are serving as force multipliers.

-The baby who had a chest tube placed and who was intubated yesterday by one of our PH OB doctors is alive and doing well at Abidin today.

-Our PH dermatologist saw 50 patients at TNI today.

7. Our 10 folks who went in to replace water run-off piping had a hot and tough day, and it will take 2 more long days to finish the

project. Other than a 'handful' of blisters, however, they are in great spirits. (No pun intended here, certainly.)

Finally, Commodore Conrad Divis has a daughter who has been admitted to USUHS (US military) Medical School. In her honor, I think, he went to surgery with our orthopedic surgeons, scrubbed in, and stayed the course in the case! He may have a second career yet!

Bill McDaniel

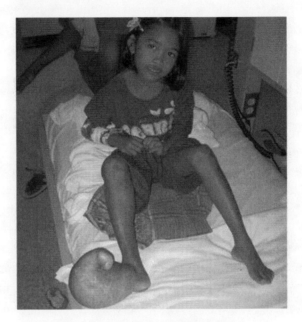

Tara with her "Elves Foot"

Subject: Sitrep Banda Aceh 10 March

We are winding down, and saying our goodbyes slowly, though it's hard to see from the numbers still being generated. Our remaining patients are doing well. The little 17 month old boy with the liver tumor is in the midst of the process that may result in his being able to go to Boston for surgery. A biopsy has revealed this to be an operable tumor, non-malignant. I found out yet again something very interesting about his family today. His mother, three older sisters (who were triplets) and he were racing to outrun the tsunami when he fell from the moped they were on, striking his head and leaving a tremendous wound which is still in the process of healing 2 months+ after the event. He was rescued, somehow, but his three sisters perished. He is the only family left to his delightful Mom, who smiles constantly and delights in being around the staff with her big-eyed son.

CDR Clark, NC, who has the lead at the nursing school and in the BLS courses, said today, quietly, "Saturday is my last day, and it will be a very sad day for me; I'll miss my kids." I expect she speaks for most of us.

1. 573 patients were seen between the two hospitals today, and optometry finished off in style. They ran out of glasses. They saw 516 patients today, and in the time here have seen almost 5300 patients, giving away almost 5000 pairs of glasses. Not bad. An Indonesian TV station showed up at the Optometry clinic and interviewed our optometrist; he got the chance to tell what they had done, and to announce that we are out of glasses and will not return. Otherwise, there could easily be 400 or so patients waiting...impatiently...at the clinic tomorrow. 2 patients went home from Mercy, and none were admitted. We had 2 Indonesian physicians and 6 Aussie Aid physicians and nurses aboard for the day. We did 5 surgeries today.

2. LCDR Harmon, US Coast Guard, again went to ICRC Hospital today to coordinate our efforts with them. Along with CDR Karen McDonald, he has been the primary person doing the very difficult job of screening all the hundreds of would-be patients to allow aboard only those patients we should be seeing. They have coordinated closely with ICRC, and are responsible for them accepting our patients from the ship when we leave.

3. The clinical team, headed by CDR Clark and CDR Comlish, worked with 68 nursing students today on burn trauma, and issued 22 BLS certificates.

4. Engineering continued to paint the workshop, overhauled another air compressor, and helped work on the pipeline today.

5. 10 corpsmen worked all day again on ditch digging in preparation to laying a pipeline tomorrow.

6. The UNICEF team continued their educational efforts today, with great success.

7. At TNI Hospital, 23 nurses were educated in orthopedic case care today.

-The Mexican surgeons were there today, and along with their nurses will take over from us on Monday.

-Our PH internist went to TNI today, and remarked on how much better the nursing skills of the nurses there were now that our folks have been working so closely with them

-A big need for the future, if someone in the US gets the chance, is to return and teach an EMT (emergency medical technician) course here. They would love to have it, and could use it to great advantage.

8. CAPT Llewellyn and I went to the Indonesian Provincial Health Office today for the medical meeting. He gave a summary of everything we have done to date, thanking all present for allowing us to work alongside them in this incredible effort.

-WHO and the Thailand government are hosting a medical lessons learned from the tsunami the first week in May in Phuket; there will be a section devoted to the civil-military interaction and its future. Someone from Mercy should definitely attend. The head of WHO asked me today if we could make sure that we were represented. I told him I would pass this along for consideration.

We continue to evaluate patients we might be able to assist greatly in the short time we have here. Tomorrow we will do a CT on an eye tumor, and will evaluate a 7 year old girl with a fracture around the elbow.

Bill McDaniel

We did not send anyone from Mercy to Phuket for the conference. I think someone from Hawaii attended. Not good enough. You need to send people who have been on site working the issues. Someone from Mercy should have been included as the key spokesman for our side.

Subject: Sitrep Banda Aceh 11 March

"Hi, people, our song is ended.
That's all what we presented.
We will go home.
The time has come."
The last verse of a song and native dance done by 8 men today from the Kanaivasu Foundaion which supplies psychological support for children of the tsunami, at the conclusion of our psych team's extensive efforts here in Banda Aceh. They then concluded with:

"This Song and Dance is dedicated by the Staff of Kanaivasu Foundation Aceh

To the USNS Mercy Corps,

For their kind hearts and generosity,

for their sincerity and warmth,

for their love and friendship in helping our people and our land,

Naggroe Aceh Darrusalam."

I was talking today with a reporter from my home island in Washington state; she has been in Aceh for most of the last 4 years. There was a young Aceh man with her, and as she and I shook hands good-by, he suddenly placed his hand on my arm and talked softly for a while. She translated that he just wanted to express the profound thanks of all the Aceh people for America being here to help them. He then placed his hand over his heart and gently grasped my hand.

These are the sort of quiet thanks we all are receiving these last few days. They don't make it any easier to leave.

No numbers today; it was not a numbers kind of day. It is a Hindu holiday and there was little to do ashore. The Chaplain and his team continue to work on digging a ditch and laying a new pipeline at Abidin; they will finish tomorrow. We are looking at how to do a major toy distribution over the next couple of days also.

Dr Purdy, ophthalmologist from PH, operated on an eye tumor of a patient today; he thinks it went well. This is the kind of thing we can do quickly, and which will make a lifetime of difference to the individual.

Dr. Rus, Director of Abidin, signed a letter today helping our liver tumor patient, Fadhil, another step along his way to Boston for definitive care. Dr. Vicky Noble from PH will travel to Jakarta with Fadhil and his father to finish the paperwork and then accompany him to Boston. This kid now is King of Ward I...and Tara, the amputee, is the definite Queen of the same ward. It is their domain, and they do hold court.

A small team went to TNI today and continued to work with them.

We had a media crew aboard yesterday and today. The ABC crew from Philly had a great time interviewing their PH folks and others. I then accompanied them ashore for 4 hours today. They initially felt that by flying over the tsunami zone and shooting from a helo was 'good enough.' I explained to them that they had to be there, so we obtained a van and drove out among the ruins.

We stopped in the middle of the devastation and walked across the rubble, silently. Red flags were all around, marking bodies. The anchor, Anita Brikman, looked around for a while, then said, "How can anyone capture this on film? How can we explain to the people at home the total destruction here? We can't. We can't begin to do this justice." A man walked out to us and asked to speak. Anita interviewed him. He led her and the camera over to where his house used to be, and explained what happened. When Anita came back, she looked stricken, and for at least the second time today had tears running down her face. "He lost his whole family. They ran and ran from the tsunami, but couldn't outrun it. He was the only survivor. And the rest of the world thinks this is over?"

They ran live clips from the ship in Philly today, and will likely have more footage to show over the next few days. They also spent an hour with the EPMU6 team at IOM filming and interviewing, and will forward that film to the ABC affiliate in Hawaii.

Tomorrow will be a busy day, our last really busy day. Then come the good-by's.

Bill McDaniel

The episode with the film crew from Philly was interesting. Initially they had no desire to really get on the ground in the severely affected area; they had, indeed, flown over it and got great shots to show. However, shots from the air did not do it justice. I had probably been on the "beach" in the totally destroyed area a dozen times by now, and had shed tears every time I went. As we walked around, with Anita and the cameraman and the light man in sort of a daze, we saw little details. A Minnie Mouse doll leaning on the foundations of a house with a metal piece piercing its chest. Steps leading to…nowhere. Crushed appliances. Cars rolled up into small balls of metal. And, everywhere, foundations of what used to be lovely homes and small red flags on bamboo poles.

The cameraman, a fellow about 50 from Puerto Rico, asked if I would walk with him up a small hill so he could get a panoramic shot. We got to the top and I gazed off into the distance at the total and complete devastation. As I talked to him I turned and saw that he had just laid his camera down and was standing with tears running down his face.

"Admiral, I have been doing this for 30 years. I have filmed scenes from disasters all over the world, both man-made and from natural disasters. This is the first time I have ever tried to film something that I just cannot comprehend. I just can't."

Since then I expect he has been to Katrina in New Orleans, Haiti, Pakistan, and most recently, Japan following their incredible tsunami. I doubt that he was able to comprehend those events either. I certainly can't. And, I'm sure he cried; after all, he was human, and that is what we do when overwhelmed. Luckily, we usually manage to get back up and meet the next challenge.

Subject: Sitrep Banda Aceh 14 March

A note from a patient today:

"To all doctors and nurses in USNS Mercy. I dare myself to write this letter to you. It is because I want to thank you very much for taking care my sister in this ship, since our arrival, the recovery period to the departure of us.

I remember when you had changed my sister's clothes with great and sincere love. We cannot pay you for everything that you have given. May God bless you doctors and all nurses in the Mercy ship for helping and supporting my sister. I cannot say anything to you, but I can only pray that God will pay for your patience and support in curing my sister. When I arrived in this ship, in my loneliness, I kept wondering whether my sister would get better.

I really love my sister since she give up her live for her sisters and brothers. Probably, she is never happy in her life--before she arrived in this ship. The only happiness for her was when she had two children. However now she has her second happiness which is health. I am now very happy while I was here.

Once again, thanks to all doctors and nurses. If you have a chance to visit Banda Aceh, please come to our small house."

Sort of difficult to say it any better than that

.1. Light days now. All patients and families went ashore, except Fadhil, the liver tumor patient who is going to Boston. Leave taking was tough on everyone. Nurses, social workers, doctors, and patients crying. Our 28 year old arm amputee whose leg our orthopods saved was lying on his bunk in a corner, quietly crying. He sat up and shook hands, and said thanks, tears still flowing. Tough on them, tough on us.

2. We had 9 visitors aboard today. Between yesterday and today all the translators on shore and drivers came to the ship, and loved their visit. They had not been aboard before this.

3. Dr. Vicky Noble and our Jag officer, and Fadhil and his Mother, spent 8 hours today getting passports. Sort of difficult when

you have absolutely no paperwork to start with. One of our translators typed up birth certificates for them. The village elder and Dr. Rus of Abidin wrote letters for them. And, we put a large bandage around Fadhil's head to push things along a little bit, though he really does not need it. 8 hours of bureaucracy later Fadhil and his Mother have passports. Tomorrow, to Jakarta.

-While at the police station Dr. Noble did house calls, examining and treating a foot wound on a policeman, from the tsunami, and examining a pregnant woman there. (When you need the police permission to do something it certainly helps when the chief needs a physician!)

4. Our Comril (community relations) team under the Chaplain passed out 6 large boxes of toys at an IDP camp today. About 300 people were on hand for the event, and were quite eager to get up close to the truck.

5. A small team went to TNI today. 6 OB patients were seen, 15 ortho, and one general surgery. Dr. Secriest did an external fixation on an infected femur fracture, using a Black and Decker drill, and worked under flashlights for the last hour of the case. He noted that it was one of the most difficult cases he has done.

Tomorrow will be spent getting EPMU6 (preventive medicine team) and their equipment back aboard.

Everyone at Abidin was aware that today was our last day there. Little boys were coming up and giving coins to our personnel there 'for their boys.' Patients' families showed up en mass to bid farewell, hugging all of our folks ashore. They were sad. So were we.

It's been a worthwhile trip...from every aspect.

Bill McDaniel

As you might imagine, these were tough days for all of us. Lots of tears, lots of fear at so much left undone...not from lack of effort, just lack of time.

A note about the arm amputee whose femur fracture we worked on. This was a case we initially almost did not do. Two years ago this poor guy had been living up in the mountains with his family; he had inadvertently got caught in the crossfire between the GAM and TNI. He lost an arm and sustained a femur fracture in that event. His femur fracture was operated upon and a plate placed over the fracture.

For safety he decided to move his family down to the seaside...where the tsunami got him! His major injury was when something slammed into his old femur fracture, causing a penetrating injury into the not-really-healed fracture site, which then got infected. When we saw him our doctors initially said there was nothing they could do for him; after all, he needed surgery to remove the plate, then 6 weeks of IV antibiotic treatment before an attempt was made to rod the femur fracture. And, we were preparing to leave.

However, it was also recognized that if we did not do something for him he would likely lose his femur, making him a double amputee, a devastating condition in that society. So, we went ahead with the initial surgery, aggressively treating him with IV antibiotics and tubes irrigating the fracture site. Shortly before we were due to leave we rodded his femur...without signs of a subsequent infection. We kept him until the last minute on antibiotics, and he was removed from the ship as we began our journey home. I think he truly understood what we had done for him.

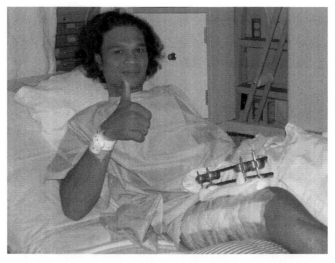

Last patient aboard as his femur fracture heals

Subject: Sitrep 70 miles South of Banda Aceh, 16 March

I expect this will be my last sitrep. I hope everyone has understood that this has been a people thing vice a numbers thing.. As such, the people stories were an essential part of it. If by chance any one passed over them to get to the numbers, I think you missed the most important part of this evolution. The numbers are impressive enough, but tell only a fraction of the story.

We went into Banda Aceh this morning to say our formal good byes. Our initial stop was at Abidin University Hospital, where Dr. Holt of Project Hope, CAPT Llewellyn, and Commodore Divis gave gifts and good words to Dr. Rus. He was gracious and clearly touched, but remained as in control as he has been since the day after the tsunami when he left his ruined home and absent family and returned to work. He thanked us very warmly, spent a few moments with CDR McDonald, who has been his primary contact every day, and we went on our way with promises of continued contact and relationships in the future. He is clearly anxious for that to continue.

Our next stop was IOM (International Organization for Migration), where CDR Banks (our uniformed interpreter and general liaison) was well received. Inasmuch as he had already said his good byes yesterday, he did not want to go through that again! We went through the same going away ritual there, and departed.

At our next stop, TNI Hospital, we were initially greeted by the Director of Nursing, a COL wearing a .45. He asked us to wait in a room; any time a nurse wearing a gun asks me to do something, I am quick to comply. After a while the CO of the hospital, his Chief of Staff, and the Head Nurse returned, where we again went through the process of presentations. As the Chief of Staff started to respond, he broke down crying, followed immediately by the Head Nurse. Two people with .45's crying worried me a little to the point of distraction, but they recovered. LCDR Erickson-Hurt, who has been the primary point of contact with them, tried to speak and met with equal difficulty. All were clearly very upset at our departure. They have excellent replacements for us in the Mexican doctors, but they appear not to see that yet. We were pleased to note our many boxes of donated medical supplies had arrived.

We then proceeded to the TNI military headquarters. MG Bombang was gone on a personal emergency, and his deputy, BG Heryadi, did the honors. Again, the same format, and BG Heryadi rose to speak. He is a line officer, a Raider (trained at Ft. Bragg), and as he spoke tears again started flowing from him. He spoke of expanded relations between our countries, and expressed genuine thanks for our compassion for the Indonesian people. When we left, the entire TNI staff, and all of our drivers, saluted as we departed and stood and waved as long as we could see them from the helo.

I don't know what the actual expense of this Mercy mission was, but my guess is that we have spent far more on many other ventures, with far less return. What would you pay to turn around the perceptions of the largest Moslem nation in the world toward the US?

Whatever we paid for Lincoln and Mercy's presence, I think we got excellent value for the money spent.

Someone must take the lead at this point in building on this. First is establishing lessons learned and recommendations. Then, in my opinion, it is important to again engage the international UN agencies..WHO and UNICEF..as well as other NGO's, in an ongoing dialogue in building on the foundation established here.

Finally, Project Hope. We had a long meeting this afternoon on their participation in this. I think their participation has been an unparalleled and unqualified success. They have added immeasurably to the success of this mission. I urged the Project Hope personnel on Mercy to do 'lessons learned' and submit them through their leadership. While we did great together, this is a first effort, and clearly could be done better in the future. We need to find out those improvement methods, then put them into practice. I firmly feel that this is the model for the future for responding to DR/HA (Disaster relief/Humanitarian assistance) missions...and not only on our floating platforms. Why not in cases where we respond to major disasters inland?

It has been an honor for all of us to have been involved in this endeavor.

Bill McDaniel

Subject: Last report on Aceh, 17 March 2005

It's 3:00 AM, somewhere in the Malacca Straits between Indonesia and Malaysia, and I am unable to sleep. I have been lying in bed thinking of the events of the past day, the past months. I have been thinking of the farewells we said yesterday to the various peoples and hospitals we have been working with for the last 6 weeks. Of senior Indonesian doctors and nurses, and even an Indonesian TNI General, who came to tears as they bid us good bye. They weren't embarrassed by their tears; they stopped for a moment in their presentations and wiped them away, but continued on. And trust me on this point...the tears were not all on their side. There were tears enough for all of us. And, as our helicopter climbed away from our final stop at TNI Army headquarters, their entire staff came outside to wave good bye to us, and we to them. They were still waving when we banked away and headed back to Mercy. I have been thinking of the wholesale tears shed by everyone on Mercy, and by all the patients and their families, as they have departed over the last several days. Of our 28 year old patient with the amputated arm, and upon whom we have worked furiously trying to save his leg so he can continue as the wage earner in his life. He was among the last to leave as we continued pouring antibiotics into him until the final moments to calm his infection. On his last day aboard I wandered back to his bunk in the far corner of Ward 1, to find him lying on his side, tears ever so quietly flowing down on his pillow.

He saw me standing there, sat up, grasped my hand for a moment, and in his newly found English murmured "Thank you." Not to me, but to us. To America. I have been thinking about Habibah, our little 8 month old baby whom I wrote about last time. We could not save her, and she died shortly after we took her back to Abidin Hospital so she could be on Indonesian soil in her final moments, something so very important to these proud people. She was accompanied by her Mom, and the doctor and nurses who have been with her constantly since 25 February. They poured out all their wonderful care and all their love, but it wasn't enough for this little girl, so she went the way so many thousands of her countrymen have gone in the last several months. We tried, but all the miracles of this miraculous ship and its people can't save everyone. But, we tried.

I've been thinking about the quiet but powerful speech one of our interpreters gave two nights ago to all the Project Hope folks and others of us in attendance. In her talk she explained thus:

"You have been treating the poorest people of Aceh for these past weeks, and you have reached out to them with respect, and humility, and have honored them. You have been kind to them, and have laughed with them, and always have treated them with the utmost tenderness and love. All of Indonesia knows this. Do you understand now why 70% of the Indonesian people think well of America?"

I have been thinking about friends from home who have questioned me about the expense of this mission. I don't know how much it has cost, but it certainly is in the millions of dollars. Could not that money have been better spent elsewhere? I doubt that it could. We have spent an incredible amount of the money...well intended always... on far less efforts, and almost never in modern days with the effect we have had here. How much would you pay to completely turn around the perception of the largest Moslem country in the world in these times? My feeling is this. However much was spent keeping USS Abraham Lincoln and USNS Mercy out here has been money so well spent we can't imagine the ultimate impact of it.

Several different Indonesians have expressed with amazement the thought of the largest and most powerful country in the world coming in leading with our heart and our compassion...rather than our muscle. They simply could not comprehend this before it happened. Perhaps we could not either. I have thought about the unique relationships we have engaged in here.

Working side by side with UN agencies who only 3 months ago could not bear he thought of working with any military, much less that from America. With the Aussies, the Germans, the Yemeni, the Japanese, the Swedes and the Norwegians, the Pakistanis...to name just a few. With the NGO's on the ground. Teaming with Project Hope aboard ship in a most wonderful and professional relationship whereby everyone has benefited. Why in the world can't we do this every time? Indeed, why not? Oh, I'm sure there are manifest reasons that we will all find to retreat to our former relationships, but the fact remains that we all know it is possible to come together in a common cause, in a most harmonious way.

We can do it again, and will. Once we have seen how something can be, we just can't turn our back and walk away from it. If we try, the memories of what has been, and what can be, will return over and over until we finally do it right once again. At the bottom of all this, always, are the people of Indonesia. Of Sumatra.

Of Aceh. Everything comes back to them. They initiated this coming together through their tragedy, and they were the catalyst for all that has happened since then. All of us here think about them almost constantly; they have become part of our families, and we part of theirs, I think. Their families are a lot larger than ours, deliberately. They share all with each other.

If you have read this far, I expect you will not mind my sharing my last thoughts about them.

To our Friends from Aceh, Selamat pagi. Good morning. Hello, people of Aceh.

Selamat detang. You welcomed us. We came to help, if we can. We came to assist you, where we can. We came to observe, and to learn from you, if you will allow it. We see your gentleness, your honor, your dignity, and most of all, your sense of community. We see you support each other when times are bad, and we see you rejoice in each other when news is good. We see your incredible resilience in the face of overwhelming tragedy. We see you greet and embrace each other as family, gaining ever more strength in the process. How do you do it? How do you wear your smiles so graciously? You have lost over 200,000 of your friends, your family, your countrymen, your lives. How do you not only keep smiling, but extend your selves to welcome us, to thank us?

Ma'af. We are sorry. That we cannot do more. That we would find it almost impossible to do what you do with such gentleness and grace. To carry on. To treasure what we have left, rather than endlessly grieving over what we have lost. To take another step. And another. And to look at tomorrow instead of looking at yesterday and collapsing in grief...with the immensity of it all.

Ma'af. We are sorry. As we look upon this ruined Aceh coastline, as we look at the red flags that dot every inch of the devastation...knowing that each flag represents someone loved who is forever gone...as we hear the stories of each of you, one by one. Families all gone. Friends, homes, cars, possessions....all gone. How do you go on? How do you find this strength? How can you smile and thank us? How do you face tomorrow with such...acceptance? I don't even know the words to be able to ask the question of how you have come to be who you are.

We have loved you, people of Aceh. We have helped all we can, and in the immensity of what you face, our help seems pitifully small. Raindrops in the ocean, perhaps. Or more aptly, one tear in a sea of tears.

But you say "Makasih." Thank you. And smile, and gently grasp our hands, and touch your hearts, and in doing so, touching our hearts. You say thank you. Makasih. It should be...and is...the other way around. Because we have gained so much more from this than we can ever possibly have given.

We have seen the touch of God, I think. On you. On your families. On your community.

Kami terima kasih. We thank you.

Selamat tinggal, people of Aceh. Good bye. We will certainly never forget you, ever. You thank us for helping, for reaching out and touching your lives. Well, our gentle friends, if we have touched you, you have slam dunked us. If you remember us fondly, we will remember you with pride at having been allowed the honor of knowing you, of being allowed to...briefly...touch your lives and seeing the wonder and goodness of them. As you face the future with your joyful smiles and a helping hand for your brothers and sisters, allow us to cry for you...just a little. You may not need it, but it helps us. For our many friends whom we have had the honor of treating, thank you. You have healed us more than we could ever do for you. For Jubal, and Elisa, Tara, and Pebbles, and Iqbal. For wonderful Maknawiah, our resident artist, and Fadhil, our 17 month old with a liver tumor. Zahrul, our little burn patient. Bashri, Muhammad Nasir, Nasir..my barber, and a wonderful guitar player, little Isna Basir, Sabrina, Wahyu Firmanda, our first little appendicitis patient, and the only person after the losses of the tsunami his father has left. Firmansyah, regaining strength after your brain abscess. Tiny Ainatul with your big smile. And, little Habibah, whom we loved but could not save. For these and so many others who have passed through and changed our lives forever.

Kami terima kasih, from all of us.
Sampai jumpa lagi. Until we meet again.

Bill McDaniel

Nias Island following tsunami; bank roof sits on the ground

Chapter 11

Geez, THE END of the preceding chapter sounded like…well, the end of the adventure.

Nah, not a chance!

Mercy arrived back in Singapore to off-load the civilians and excess military medical folk, intent on resuming her visit throughout the Indonesian islands and delivering great care to other needy folk. We all had a nice party in Singapore, visited Raffle's bar and had Singapore Slings, and went our separate ways, returning to the jobs we all had in civilian life.

I went to Hawaii (someone has to do it) to report out to the senior staff officers there. I speak slowly, so it took me several days to report out. (I'm old, not stupid.) I told the senior line officers there most of what I have noted throughout the chapters thus far. They agreed with the effectiveness of our efforts, and also agreed that involvement of civilian medical folks in these efforts had major benefits for all. As I have noted previously, we don't really do lessons learned all that well, however. It seems that we are so big, so diverse, so multi-talented, that when we go to a disaster we almost always do an outstanding job. Perhaps doing it 5 or 10% better is just not worth the extra effort.

I ruminated a lot while in Hawaii those few days. It's not easy shaking off the effects of 2+ months of dealing with such people as we dealt with, with such astounding problems and grand (and little) solutions. I was unaccountably emotional for some reason. I visited friends who had received the six or so reports I had sent out to my email list; they had a gathering of their friends in and asked me if I would read them my missives. I started to do so, standing in the middle of the living room, and somewhere in the second page or so I had to stop. Probably had too much wine.

I talked with other friends whose kids had been gathering money with various sales events to send to the children of Aceh. They asked me who they should send the money to. I suggested that the father take his two children with him to Aceh and deliver the money personally, seeing what there was to see there. I hope they did so; those kids will never forget the event if they did. If they sit in that blue UNICEF tent and talk with those most wonderful orphans they will receive something in return that will be ever so valuable to them all their lives. We all did.

Finally, on about 24 March I arrived home to my wife, Shirley.

A day passed, or two, and I heard about a massive earthquake that had struck just south of the previous one. This one was an 8.7, and had caused massive damage to Nias Island, an island immediately north of the epicenter of the DEC 26th quake. Nias had not been damaged in the DEC quake, but subsequent studies revealed that about 30,000 homes and businesses had been destroyed that March morning, with 1800 or so lives lost. One of the structures severely damaged was the only hospital on the island, in the capital city of Gunungsitoli.

As I was reading about the quake my phone rang. The number 2 Admiral in the Pacific Fleet headquarters was on the phone.

"How soon can you be in Singapore?"

Now I had already checked this, and told him I could be there by midnight the next day. I had a feeling we were going back. The Minister of Health in Jakarta had called the US Ambassador and asked him if Mercy could return for a while to help in Nias, inasmuch as the hospital there was severely damaged. Mercy had just turned around and started steaming back at full speed. (Realizing "full speed" is a misnomer when 16 knots almost shakes her to pieces!)

So, I returned; I had not even gotten adjusted to stateside time yet, so little readjustment was required to start back.

I arrived back on Nias Island via helicopter from Singapore, and immediately started helping our comms (communications) folks set up living quarters (in a tent, of course) and our comms tent. This was all done in the town square, immediately adjacent to a collapsed bank. The only thing intact from the bank was the very ornate roof…which was setting on the ground atop the rubble of the bank. The island was really a mess, with thousands of homes totally crumbled, in many cases with families still inside them. The hospital had extensive damage, but the ER was still up and running. Most patients were in beds outside the rooms, under cover in open hallways.

One of the only really good things from our point of view was that Nias Island is a Christian enclave, while Banda Aceh had been all Moslem. The difference? Well, in a word, beer.

The temperature was 90+ by 7:00 AM, and just got hotter. As I walked around the first day with a friend (CDR Banks) who spoke Bahassa, we passed a little market, still intact. As I looked in I saw what appeared to be liter bottles of Bintang beer. Hot of course, but liquid. I asked the proprietor through the interpreter if he sold cold beer? No, not really. I told him that a lot of Americans were just over the horizon; they like their beer cold, especially when the temperature was as hot as it was on Nias. When I went back by the store the next day there was an upright freezer there. The owner motioned me in, opened the freezer door, and showed me about 50 liters of very, very cold beer. He opened one for me. Little ice crystals formed inside; it tasted better than most any beverage I had ever consumed! He did a great business for the next month or so.

While we had MRE rations to eat, most of us living ashore went up the street to a small tarp-covered café about a block away. The building the café had been in was destroyed, so they improvised. I had almost every meal there. Nasi goring. That is a staple in Asia, no matter what country you are in. It is basically fried rice with things thrown in. Whatever is available, I guess. Always eggs. Sometimes ham, or bacon, some onions, unknown spices, sometimes meat I did not desire to identify. It all tasted great! A large plate of that with two huge cups of wonderful coffee for breakfast cost about $.85. Not bad, not bad at all!

We had been on the island for only a day or so when a 6.8 aftershock hit. Pretty impressive, but we were not concerned about our tent falling on us. However, within moments hundreds, perhaps thousands, of terrified locals were running away from the waterfront 2 blocks away, extremely afraid that the earthquake might trigger another tsunami. It didn't, but those folks were quite jittery; it was impossible to blame them. Of course, if a tsunami had occurred, there we were sitting in a tent. Perhaps we could have floated out on the radios?

Mercy appeared on the horizon, helos started flying in, and we got to work. All land lines had been ruined by the quake, and we were dependent on our comms tent for all communication with the ship. Of interest, I thought, was an American crew that came in from somewhere and erected an antenna on top of one of the intact buildings. Suddenly we had Internet with a wireless connection. Sort of odd; no phone service, but excellent Internet service! We communicated with Mercy as much by Internet as we did by our phone detachment efforts.

A most sobering moment came within the first day or so of my arrival on Nias. I was in a US helo doing a survey of the island, our first real view of the damage it had sustained, which was immense. As we flew over a village I saw the site of what appeared to be a plane crash in a field, with wreckage still around and a large charred area surrounding the fuselage of a burned-out helo. I asked our pilot what had happened?

Well, unfortunately, several of our Australian medical colleagues, both doctors and nurses, had been preparing to leave Banda Aceh when the March 28 earthquake hit. Their helo had detoured to do the same thing we were doing, a survey. It developed mechanical trouble and crashed, killing all personnel aboard. Just an absolutely superb crew of wonderful people who had been on scene for several months…gone, suddenly. It just did not seem real, and truly brought home to us the danger of some of the activities we routinely engaged in.

Again, I hope we never forget those wonderful Aussies.

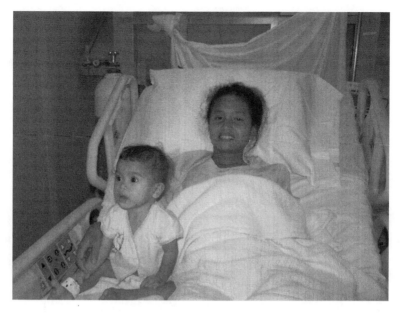

Dua baby sitting Putri Dua

Chapter 12

Subject: Sitrep Gunungsitoli, Nias 6 April 2005

Aｎｄ YOU THOUGHT I had finished.

Today was our first full day of sending medical teams into the capital city of Nias Island, Gunungsitoli. As we attended a meeting at the Provincial Health Offices at 0830 with a small group of NGO's, the lights in the building were out, having been out since the earthquake. Midway through the meeting we felt a small quake, whereupon the lights suddenly all came on. It was an interesting sensation; I'm not sure if that is a positive omen or not, but will choose to interpret it as one.

We had teams at the helo landing field near downtown (a soccer field, as usual), at the PHO (Public Health Offices) (Pendopo), at the airport (9 miles as the crow flies from Pendopo, but about 20 death-defying driving miles away), and at the local hospital. I would reveal its name, but none of us has figured out what it is called yet.

The highlight of this first day of work ashore was a visit to the airfield to evaluate several patients. The French medevac personnel had done an excellent job by the time we arrived, and we only had one patient to medevac from there, a suspected compound ankle fracture. While we were evaluating the patients, a physician from the next door Russian tent hospital asked us to evaluate a sick 17 month old child, and Dr. Braner, the Project Hope pediatric intensive care specialist, went with him while we finished up. We went to the Russian hospital soon thereafter, to find Dr. Braner feverishly attempting to start an IV in the tiny arm of an extremely ill and toxic child who was also severely dehydrated. He somehow found a vein and got an IV going. The child was having extreme difficulty breathing, and Dr. Braner stated that the child was only moments to an hour or two from dying. We called for a medevac while he continued to work on the child, talking all the while to his ill patient. It was interesting, and an education, to watch him work. We got a quick medevac, and the child is now on a respirator in the ICU aboard Mercy. Dr. Braner noted after admission here that he has never seen all blood work so out of whack as it is on this kid. More as we go forth in this case. But, as of right now, Mercy, some good helo work, and Dr. Braner's skills are the only reasons this child is alive tonight.

Other impressions while driving around today. There are a lot of homes and businesses flattened totally. We all think it is amazing the death toll was not higher, but were told that everyone ran from their homes when the quake started, headed for the surrounding hills in the event of another tsunami. Also, almost all of the homes have pallets in front of them. Virtually no one sleeps indoors at night, for fear of another quake. Having felt two small ones today, we share that hesitation of spending a lot of time indoors. We observed bodies being removed from one site as we drove past. From the looks of the buildings, I suspect they will find quite a few more over the next few weeks.

We admitted 3 patients today. The ankle problem, the child above, and a young woman with appendicitis whom we will operate upon tomorrow.

We visited the Russian hospital, and in talks with their commander were told that they are leaving in 4 days. They asked if we could assume the care of their 230 patients. I told them we were not setting up a primary care base here, and were strictly acting as a tertiary referral hospital, and could only take patients needing tertiary care at this time. They understood and agreed. I was later told that the Japanese are bringing in 5 doctors to do primary care, and the Indonesian Red Crescent is coming in to do primary care as well, so they should be covered.

The comms teams were busy testing communication capabilities ashore today, and found that they are very poor. The Indonesian cell system *seems* to be working, but no one on the island can get a call through. We relied on Iridium phones and com sat phones for communication between shore and Mercy, and on radios for comms between groups on shore. The Cell-Tel system worked at times, but inasmuch as Mercy had to keep moving for security reasons, communications via that system are spotty and poor at best. We are not going to be able to depend on cell phone comms for patient referrals, and will have to set up several loci for communications and screeners each day ashore to allow referral NGO's to have access to us.

We identified a command and control site on which we can erect a tent and maintain a small detachment as soon as we are allowed by higher authority to keep a small detachment ashore. This is in front of the City Hall, co-located with tents from a number of other countries. It is a very public, and apparently a very secure area. We neither saw nor heard any evidence of any force protection problems on Nias.

Several NGO's, specifically IOM, International Red Cross, and Oxfam, want to work closely with our Preventive Medicine

(EPMU6) personnel. Mercy Singapore doctors (Mercy is another worldwide NGO) met with us and we went over procedures with them.

We are working at establishing a format by which we will be referred patients from shore. This is complicated somewhat by the absence of reliable communications. We have a tentative plan in place. The Provincial Health Office is not interested in being involved in the referral process, but want a report on the patients we have aboard each morning. Mark Jackson of AusAid has volunteered to be the clearing house for referrals. We will likely take him up on this.

We had a very positive interaction with the district hospital director, and Dr. Polifka of Project Hope and CAPT Craig Powell made rounds there, identifying a number of orthopedic cases that will need surgery over the next week or so. They saw 18 patients, most of whom may be admitted to Mercy soon.

Tomorrow we will send in about the same number of personnel, and at 10:00 am or so Mercy will make the 80 mile transit to the mainland to pick up the next wave of Project Hope volunteers. About 1/3 of the current group aboard Mercy now are repeats from one of the earlier tours here, and seeing them greet the crew and each other is a delightful experience. They all act like they are back where they love to be at this point in time.

I'm proud, as well, to be involved in this effort.

Bill McDaniel

Medevac helos were scarce. Our Blackhawk helos are not great for going into villages to pick up patients; a much smaller air frame is needed. Ours tend to blow all the houses away, creating some angst among the home owners. Mark Jackson of AusAid, a New Zealander, became an incredibly valuable referral agent for us. He had access to all the smaller helos available, and understood that we were there for the complex cases, not immediate treatment for bumps and bruises, and not chronic convalescent cases. He very

156

effectively screened them for us, and in turn we trusted his judgment when he said someone needed our services.

I would return to Mercy about every 3 days to shower and sleep in air conditioned comfort for a night. The rest of the time I spent ashore.

Subject: Sitrep Nias 7 April

First, a follow up. 17 month old Petrus Tan, the tiny baby we brought to Mercy from the Russian tent hospital yesterday, is doing much better. She is still on a respirator, but all chemistries and blood gasses are looking good. Dr. Bruner is walking around the ship with a big smile. As I walked through the Russian compound today, two nurses came out to ask me how she was doing. This was an interesting task, inasmuch as they know about as much English as I do Russian. However, when you are talking about a sick infant, communication is easy. They were thrilled.

We have another very ill child here now. As Dr. Yoshihashi and I were talking with the Singapore Mercy physicians at their clinic (in a school) today, one of them noted that there was a patient he had not seen yet that we might look at. A 7 year old girl had a massively infected lip and face; she was toxic and in a lot of pain. We immediately started her on IV antibiotics and called someone smarter than we were to evaluate her. CDR Hummeldorf agreed with our assessment, so we medevaced her to Mercy this afternoon. Sick though the little girl was, she sat up and watched as we flew a considerable distance to meet Mercy as the ship steamed back from picking up the rest of the Project Hope personnel. She is now in the hands of some outstanding doctors, and we have high hopes for her.

We admitted two other victims of the earthquake today, a 52 year old man with a fractured femur, and a 70 year old man with a fractured femur and both arms broken. After bringing the two patients out to Mercy, with the 70 year old man's son accompanying him, we found out that father and son, and the 14 year old daughter of the son were the only members of the family to survive the collapse of their home. And, the 14 year old daughter has a fractured pelvis and is in the same hospital that we got her grandfather out of. Family and togetherness is everything here; needless to say, one of our admissions tomorrow will be a 14 year old girl with a fractured pelvis.

By the way, the name of the hospital in Gunungsitoli is…Gunungsitoli Hospital. We finally figured it out. Advanced educations do pay off occasionally.

At our 0800 meeting at the Provincial Health Office today the principal topic was Mercy. The officials of WHO and the PHO visited Mercy yesterday, and told the audience about the ship; it is very interesting hearing a description from someone like this. It makes you feel part of a very marvelous enterprise to hear them describe what they saw. They then asked if I would explain what kinds of patients we were prepared to admit, and I told them in some detail. There was no organization represented in the audience that did not come up to one of us afterward and thank us for bringing Mercy and her capabilities to assist them.

Communications are still difficult, though through communication satellites, MMarsat, and Iridium phones we manage to communicate between shore and Mercy, though not always so well between ourselves on shore. Cell phones are still worthless, so NGO's who would like to refer patients to us find it somewhat difficult to do. Therefore, we advertise the fact that we have triage officers at three sites, so that at least they will be able to come to one of those to refer patients to us.

Dr. Prolifka worked the city hospital today, and several of us worked at transferring the two patients from there to Mercy. CDR Hummeldorf went to the airport, where I joined him later. We had a lively discussion with the Russians there, who are still concerned that there will be no primary care capability at that site when they leave.

Preventive medicine is going to be very gainfully employed here. Everyone is happy to see them, building on their hard work and successes in Banda Aceh. Most folks here knew them there, and want to work with them. WHO, Surfaid, Unicef, IOM, IMC, World Food Program, and Oxfam all approached them and want to work with them in doing water testing all over Nias. They are well aware of the very sophisticated lab setup our folks have, as well as their demonstrated expertise in Banda Aceh, and want to take advantage of it. Their problem will not be finding work, but coordinating it for maximum efficiency while we are here.

We have approximately 7 patients scheduled to be admitted tomorrow, and Dr Peterson, Navy orthopedic surgeon from Japan, has a full day of surgery planned with the 4 extremity fractures we have in house now. I will be the traction apparatus for him as he nails and plates these.

We have been told that there are literally hundreds of fractures scattered around the island of Nias. With a population of 670,000, that is not surprising. Many of them are afraid to leave their villages and come to Gunungsitoli for care, but I strongly suspect that we will start seeing a steady flow of patients from them very soon. With the incredibly positive reception we have received from all the NGO's and the hospital, I suspect word will spread.

Bill McDaniel

On the first day we started doing surgery full time we only had one young orthopedic surgeon aboard. The others were en route from the states. So, I scrubbed in with the one other orthopod. We had done several cases, mostly compound fractures, and had been in the OR for 6-8 hours, when suddenly the OR door banged open.

There stood Franklin Secriest, a wonderful Navy orthopedic surgeon from San Diego Regional Medical Center. Franklin had been on board for the entire Banda Aceh visit, then had flown back to San Diego. As soon as he heard Mercy was returning to Nias Island, he applied to return.

"Admiral, sir, you are relieved!" He was standing there with a big grin, suitcase in hand. He returned moments later in scrubs and relieved me. The patients were definitely far better off in his capable hands!

Subject: Sitrep Sibolga, Sumatra 9 April

You might have noted no sitrep last night; I was ashore in Gunungsitoli. I attended the evening meeting of the NGO reps at the Provincial Health Office. It was an excellent meeting in which the assembled NGO's outlined their efforts to get tents, food, water, and medical supplies out to the people of Nias. The meeting was well run, and I was extremely impressed by the amount of help they offered each other every time a problem came up. There were a surprising number of Americans represented in all the NGO groups; that was very nice to see.

There are still lots of severely affected areas on the island, and some of the shipments into those areas are being mobbed by hungry and thirsty islanders. No crime, just hunger.

One of the surprising observations noted by all was that the island of Nias has apparently risen about 2 meters higher. There is a much wider expanse of coast line all along the West coast now, and rivers that used to be 2-3 meters deep are now only 2 feet deep at low tide. So, the NGO's are taking advantage of this by driving from village to village along a formerly impassable beach.

The governor of Nias has outlined a timed approach to the efforts here. The first phase, rescue, ends at 2 weeks, which is tomorrow. The second phase is recovery, lasting another 2 weeks, then comes reconstruction. In walking around the waterfront last night, where much of the damage occurred, I noted that they are in all three phases at once, and pursuing their goals with some vigor.

This morning I brought a "stable" baby (Benny) with pneumonia back to Mercy, a 13 mo. old boy. As an orthopedic doc, sick kids scare me as much as they do most of you. This little boy went sour within 15 minutes, and there I sat at the soccer field waiting for the helo, with no one but the crying father, 30-40 curious locals, and 2 Indonesian photographers recording it all. I held this little kid, begging him not to die, bathing him continually, for 2 hours and 15 minutes, until the helo got to us and we got back to the ship. I just knew he was going to die in my arms; I didn't care for the feeling. I tried Dana Braner's trick of talking nonstop to the kid all the time I was holding him. (Dana is the Project Hope doc I praised in my last report for another save.) I don't know if my talking did the kid any good, but it sure emotionally exhausted me. Finally, when we arrived back on Mercy, Dana and our Navy pedi doc, Wendy, took over...thank God. There was Dana, only 2 hours from leaving Mercy for home, at the head of the table calmly intubating the kid while teams worked feverishly doing all the rest of the things necessary to do, all under Dana's watchful eye. I stood to the side, too physically and emotionally exhausted to get in their way, luckily. The kid is now in ICU on a respirator, extremely sick, but he has a chance to live...thanks to a great team led by Dana. A fitting end to a great doctor's Mercy adventure.

Our other patients I have mentioned? The 17 month old that we brought back 2 days ago is now laughing, taking a bottle, and on his way to recovery. Our little girl with the severely swollen face is now spending time in the play room; we are awaiting our first crayon drawing of this trip. She still has a way to go, but is clearly going to do well. And, our little 14 year old girl with the fractured pelvis now is with her father and grandfather aboard Mercy. She does not need a lot of care from us, but is benefiting greatly from the love of her family.

1. We admitted 4 patients today, including the baby noted above. We did 6 surgeries, and Dr. Polifka and Dr. Sutton, a newly arrived Project Hope ER doc, saw 10 consults at the hospital. Dr. Sutton joined me for the helo ride back to Mercy with the kid, and it took both of us on that ride to keep the kid going. Dr. Sutton notes that he never thought his first day would be so exciting.

2. We erected permanent tents (sort of) in Gunungsitoli today, and starting today will have a permanent presence there. This has already paid off in multiple calls from there to Mercy tonight, with arrangements for patient pick ups tomorrow.

3. The preventive medicine teams have a tremendous amount to offer on this island. They attended a malaria meeting today, and will start helping check for intrusion of sea water into wells tomorrow. They are working with the hospital lab, bringing samples back to Mercy for analysis, and upgrading their capabilities so they can continue to do the work when we leave. They are working on joint projects to do malaria control on Nias.

4. We started retrieving Navy and Public Health personnel this afternoon off Sibolga, and will get the rest tomorrow. Therefore, our efforts in Gunungsitoli will be minimal tomorrow, though we will send a helo for personnel exchange and to retrieve more patients.

5. The hospital is eager for our optometrists and dentists to come there and start their work, and has given us two rooms for that purpose.

We have been received phenomenally well here. Everyone knows Mercy from Banda Aceh and from the many stories in the newspapers. The people of Nias, and the NGO's as well, seem to greatly appreciate our presence and efforts, and are understanding when we cannot meet all their expectations, which happens at times. The locals smile, say "Mikasi," touch their hearts, and accept our efforts as being what we can do at the time. They continue to amaze all of us with their grace.

Bill McDaniel

As our Preventive Medicine teams and volunteers spread out over the island to help the locals rebuild their homes and infrastructure, they were met with great enthusiasm. People not only enjoyed their help, they simply enjoyed having new (and very odd) visitors in areas that never saw visitors!

Subject: Sitrep Gunungsitoli 10 April

Today was a light day...for the health care workers. Not for the support ships Niagra Falls and San Jose and HC-5 helicopter

162

squadron, however! They did all the work, and did it in a superb and safe fashion, as they always do. They moved 116 passengers from Sibolga airport to Mercy, and at the same time supported two missions to Gunungsitoli, 80 miles away. (A little shorter actually, as the Master of the Mercy maneuvered back and forth to give them as much slack as possible.) All this was accomplished as we started the day with only one 'up' helo. So, first and foremost, I wish to pass my kudos to a great group of professionals who are supporting our mission to the max! And, the other very unsung supporters, our flight deck crew, who worked all day in blistering hot conditions.

As noted, we sent two 'sticks' to Gunungsitoli to change out our personnel who maintain a 24 hour a day presence there, and to pick up two patients to return here. We were unable to retrieve any more patients today due to the distance involved. However, our crew there tonight already has a medevac for us tomorrow morning.

Mr. Mark Jackson, the Kiwi who heads AusAid on Nias, came aboard Mercy early this morning and is still here tonight. We all met with him at length today mapping out our strategies and mechanisms to get patients referred to Mercy in the face of sketchy to absent communications on Nias. We have come up with a plan which looks like it will work well, with SurfAid covering the entire western side of the island into the hills, using a series of boats, motorcycles, and helos. SurfAid works for AusAid in this effort. The UN then sends helos out to retrieve the patients, and we have worked out what appears to be a feasible scheme to get those patients back to Gunungsitoli Hospital and to Mercy. Mark Jackson is extremely knowledgeable about conditions on Nias, and was immensely impressed at Mercy when he toured it today.

Mark discussed with us today what we already knew, and that is that Mercy is the only truly functional hospital on Nias, for a population of about 670,000. The Gunungsitoli Hospital is extremely basic, much more so than any hospital we saw in Banda Aceh. Any complex treatment is impossible. The only solution these people have for cases beyond mild infections is to call in medevacs and send the patients several hundred miles to Medan, and they are loathe to do that. There is the Russian tent hospital, treating very basic conditions. However, without a functional lab, no oxygen, and no real diagnostic capabilities of any sophistication at all, they are basically an outpatient facility, as is Singapore clinic, which is run out of a school. So, Mercy is it. We are the only medical game in town, and certainly Mercy is the most sophisticated hospital until you get to Singapore. Every NGO representative I have talked to since arriving is well aware of this fact, and Mercy's reputation for dealing with extremely complex (and less complex, of course) cases is well known. We have been welcomed here with open arms.

Now that we are fully staffed and able to maintain a full time presence in Gunungsitoli, Mark is convinced that we will be heavily utilized, and will save many lives in the coming weeks. We are eager to return to Gunungsitoli at first light tomorrow and go to work.

Another outstanding strength we have is our preventive medicine and Occupational Health Teams. There are major plans to involve them immediately, partnering with virtually every NGO on the island. And, as is usually the case, their positive effect will be felt long after Mercy departs the area. Our people have more capability and more materials to work with than exists on Nias at this time; they will be heavily utilized, starting tomorrow. They will also be working to upgrade the hospital lab; our engineers and medical repair technicians are already hard at work daily at the hospital. Everything they do virtually doubles the capabilities of the facility. We will leave it a much better hospital than it probably has ever been.

We did do 3 major orthopedic cases in the operating room today. At this time we also have 17 patients aboard, and fully expect more throughout the week. One of our orthopedic surgeons arrived from San Diego, walked with his luggage into the OR, and left about 8 hours later after having scrubbed in on some very difficult ortho cases. I expect he will sleep well tonight.

Our patients are all doing great! Specifically, the 13 month old baby I sweated over on the trip out to Mercy yesterday is going to survive, it appears. While he is still intubated and on a respirator, his blood work is looking good. He will likely be extubated in the next day or two. An interesting fact about him; he had a little sister born 5 days ago, and his father has had virtually no sleep since that time. Mom is home with the baby, and we have been trying to get word to her (they do not have a phone, and if they did have one, it would not be working) that her son has survived his first helo ride and treatment. The little baby we brought out 4 days ago looks great! And, our 14 year old girl with a pelvis fracture who we brought out to be with her only surviving family has a major infection, which would not have been found or treated had we left her in Gunungsitoli. Doing good deeds perhaps does pay off.

There is lots of interest in our presence here. We not only have credibility as the only major hospital in this part of Indonesia, but the folks here like us as much as they did in Banda Aceh. As I noted in my last sitrep from Banda Aceh, how much is it worth to have the most populous Moslem country in the world come to view us as we on Mercy have grown to view them—that is, with great respect and honor for the people of the other country? A rhetorical question, of course, because the answer is obvious. The value is incalculable. We will strive to maintain and improve that image through what we accomplish in the upcoming weeks.

Bill McDaniel

I am not amplifying a lot on these sitreps; it is just not needed. The details of making rounds in the partially destroyed local hospital, then making the hour or so drive to the other sites we are covering to make rounds there, are routine and mundane. It was hot, the roads were primitive and crowded, and the people uniformly smiling when they saw us come into the clinics. Not a lot to write about that might add to the sitreps. When the sitreps skip a day it is because I was ashore and was unable to post them.

Spending most nights ashore with a small det of enlisted personnel was a nice change from being aboard Mercy full time. After full darkness when no further visits were expected one of us would usually go over to the small market and get some ice cold Bintang beer; we would sit in the darkness in the shelter and discuss the day's events. A nice, quiet time. One evening a couple of the other officers and I went down to the TNI barracks next to the water and sat with them for a couple of hours, exchanging stories and sipping cold beer. Again, nothing earthshaking, but a definite building good will effort.

Subject: Sitrep Gunungsitoli 12 April

Business is picking up. After 12 admissions yesterday and 10 today, and 11 surgeries over the two days and many more difficult cases in our ship waiting to be operated upon, I think it is fair to say we are becoming engaged fully here. We are working closely with the UN helicopter dispatcher as he sends out his helos for medevac missions, most of which then are referred to us. In addition, there is an incredibly sharp USAID woman here who has a helo dedicated to scouring the hills and many small villages over the next 2 weeks to bring in all the earthquake related casualties. These are difficult missions. Reports come in with coordinates which turn out to be either dense jungle or open ocean, and the helos return, recalibrate, and go out searching again. They are giving themselves two weeks to complete their sweep of Nias for these patients, which coordinates very nicely with our plans for ramping up, doing all we can, then easing down as the patient flow decreases.

Our patients are doing well, and we continue to have a constant flow of sick infants arriving; our pediatricians are doing a great job with them. We have many broken bones from the earthquake which our two orthopedic surgeons are spending lots of hours on. Neurosurgery, urology, OB/GYN, and general surgery are staying just as busy.

When the 6.2 earthquake hit Simaleu yesterday, we felt it as a rolling quake lasting about 30 seconds. Very noticeable, and we were all quite happy to be sitting under a tent at that moment. There was one other aftershock at about 1600 yesterday, and none noted today.

Several doctors went ashore today. Unlike Banda Aceh, we are not running any clinics by ourselves yet, and optometry and the dentists start working tomorrow. Therefore, do not let the numbers fool you; they cannot be compared to Banda. Different circumstances entirely. Every patient we see is in consultation with local physicians and other NGO doctors, and the doctors are fully employed in trying to make rounds and see them all, bringing patients to the ship who we might be able to help. Neurosurgery saw 2 patients, orthopedics 11, OB 2, acute care 17, ophthalmology 3, general surgery 10, pediatrics 5, and urology 1.

Preventive medicine is getting busy, and will continue to get busier. Today they did a structural analysis of the hospital and the airport, finding the latter in good shape, and the former in very poor shape. They met with all the malaria workers, developing strategies with the director of the malaria control program for this area. They are going to be doing some advanced training for the other folks here. Both the TNI and the local police have offered them force protection when they travel to any location. They met with the Director for Water and Sanitation from the Ministry of Health in Jakarta, who is very interested in their efforts and wants the data they collect. They then met with the director of the hospital and reviewed admissions for the last week, finding a steady increase in diarrhea complaints upon admission. They will return to start culturing to see if there is a common organism in this mini-outbreak.

CDR Comlish (Director of Nursing on Mercy) spent the day working on discharge planning with all parties involved, including firming up procedures when a patient might die aboard Mercy. In addition, IOM is going to assume the task of getting patients we discharge back to their homes.

All the above paid off late today when a critically ill patient with multi-system infection died aboard Mercy. He had been brought to the ship yesterday near death, and was just too far gone to save. Movement to shore and procedures went perfectly, thanks to the groundwork done by CDR Comlish.

Tomorrow 2 of our engineers are going to town to start working on multiple projects; they will soon become as busy, and probably busier, than they were in Banda Aceh.

As I have noted before, we have been received here with open arms. We are the only significant medical care these folks have access to, and for many of them, seeing us will be the only medical care they will ever receive. With the aid of many partners from the UN and NGO's here, we will most definitely succeed in improving the medical health of Nias in the next few weeks.

Finally, I would like it noted that when you are sleeping on a cot ashore and awake in the middle of the night only to feel a scaly presence crossing your hand, it is not necessarily a large snake. It might be a cat licking the salt off your hand. And, in fact, in my experience it has always been so. However, it is difficult to slow your heart rate enough to fall asleep after that.

Bill McDaniel

Subject: sitrep Gunungsitoli, Nias 14 April

50 patients on Mercy, plus their relatives accompanying them. 8 in the Intensive Care Unit, with 2 very sick pediatric patients there. Several in isolation for tuberculosis. 23 surgeries yesterday and today. 119 X-rays taken as of this morning, as well as almost 400 lab studies conducted. 9 admissions today, 12 yesterday. At least half the surgeries are extremely complex, difficult cases. I just stopped one of the orthopedic surgeons in the hall, who has not rested much since arriving on board on Sunday. He said this work is extremely gratifying, and he is thrilled and honored to be here doing

it. He also said these were some of the most difficult trauma cases he has ever been involved in.

We are truly at maximum capacity at this time. The only way to get busier would be to add more personnel, open more than the two wards and one ICU, and add another operating room or two to the mix. I think we will maintain this pace for a while. In discussions ashore last night with some of the personnel doing surveys, they noted that of the 600 villages on Nias, only about 200 have been contacted by health assessment teams. There are lots more trauma cases out there waiting to be found.

One of the problems we face is the pending departure of Project Hope personnel in a week. The bulk of our nursing personnel is from them, as well as a lot of excellent doctors. Some are applying to stay until the end of this portion of the mission, though we are unsure exactly when that will be. We will start increasingly using our corpsmen, pulling them from other duties, so that they can do what they do best...care for patients.

I have been spending most of my time on shore working relations there, which is actually not a difficult process. Lack of reliable communications on the island is the biggest problem. We are doing well in that aspect.

We have identified 4 potential pediatric patients on Mercy now who need complex surgical procedures, and who could benefit greatly from care in the states. We approached the head of the Provincial Health Authority here today and asked him what his thoughts were? He noted that they did not have the money to send these kids to Jakarta for their surgeries, and would welcome a formal proposal from Project Hope for each child, outlining what is needed, where it could be obtained, and who would pay. We are in process of doing that at this time, translating the documents into the local dialect. We hope to have this approved very soon, so that we can begin the process of passport and visa applications and arrange for transfer before Mercy leaves the area.

Dental and optometry set up in a school with another NGO yesterday and today to run their clinics. As is usual, everyone wants their eyes checked. And, while the dental side of the clinic did not appear to be nearly so popular…as evidenced by the fact that parents were forcibly pushing each other and their children toward the tooth extraction chair…the optometry side was…well, wild. The crowd was out of control initially, pushing to get to the head of the line. Finally, with the aid of TNI, police, and our security personnel, order was restored and the clinics ran successfully for the rest of the day. From now on TNI and police presence will be on hand and order created before our personnel arrive. Optometry saw 175 people and handed out 160 pairs of glasses. (Patients with perfect vision were notably disappointed!) Dental saw 38 patients, pulling 57 teeth. 29 other patients involving various specialties were consulted on at the clinics and the hospital by the doctors ashore today as well.

Comrel (community relations) projects abound here. Everything needs help. The local authorities have requested that we prioritize our efforts, concentrating on schools and health facilities. (Local clinics are called Puskesmas.) Assessments were done today, and tomorrow a team will tackle cleaning up and building shelving in the hospital pharmacy, with the Public Health Service pharmacist categorizing the scattered medicines into some order.

We will then start working on a school library where all the shelving is destroyed; we will completely renovate it. (On all these projects engineers from all three ships here will be involved, as well as civmars (civilian crews of support ships) and sailors from all three.)

Finally, our third initial project will be at the nursing school, where a combined team of nurse educators and engineers will work on both the structure of the facility and the education of the students. Comrel teams will be quite active in our stay here.

Public health teams look to be extremely busy here as well. Last night I was approached by the Mayor of the southern-most province on the island, noting that they have had a significant increase in diarrhea there, and requesting our help. Our Public and

Environmental Health personnel engaged her this morning, and will start assessments tomorrow if she can get the information they need.

They met with the police chief of Nias, and the Minister of Health for Northern Nias today, mapping out where they feel our folks should concentrate their initial efforts. Police and TNI have promised to give them complete support when they go into an area. They collected and analyzed 24 water samples today from public drinking supplies, and found the vast majority to be liberally laced with various contaminants, which might explain the increase in diarrhea being reported.

The structural engineers met with the International Medical Corps rep today concerning the poor condition of the one hospital. After their report, the IMC announced that they would attempt to get funding to completely rebuild the facility. They surveyed the 2nd floor of the Department of Health building, which has been largely destroyed. They will go to Afulu and Lahewa in the North of the island to begin initial rebuilding projects early in the week.

We ended the day today with a VTC (video tele-conference) with Mass General Hospital, with the case to be reported in the New England Journal of Medicine. It was great seeing so many old friends on the other end of the VTC. The case was one you all have heard of before, the 17 year old girl, Elisa, who had the brain abscess after having 'tsunami lung disease.'

Finally, I spent quite a bit of time down on Ward 1 tonight. Amazing. Kids running and playing, even the ones with severe burn and tumor deformities. Babies were everywhere, and over to one side was an 8 day old baby with its Mom and Dad. Mom had a ruptured bladder in the delivery of her baby, so the whole family is together as she recuperates from some super reconstructive surgery. The child is resting in a most wonderful crib built by the engineers on Mercy. This thing would sell great at any outlet in the States! I hope they patented their crib work. I visited with our 13 year old whose parents and brothers and sisters were killed when their house fell in on them. She is here with her uncle and grandfather...the latter having 3 broken extremities. A woman whose leg we amputated yesterday for severe infection of the bone smiled and gently grasped my hand for a moment. Our little 17 month old with a serious heart defect was sleeping peacefully, awaiting word on whether we will be able to bring her to the States for a curative surgery. She was beautiful. In the corner I sat a moment with a very sad woman with broken legs; I found out that when her house collapsed in the earthquake 2 weeks ago her baby was killed.

As was the case in Banda Aceh, these people do not desire isolation or privacy. They bond together and support each other, and the entire ward is a family, sharing happiness and commiserating in sadness. There are no loners here; the others are always there for them. As I left the ward, I saw a 7 year old boy asleep on his bunk, and his father lying on a mattress on the floor beside him, arm up on the bunk holding his son's hand as they slept.

Bill McDaniel

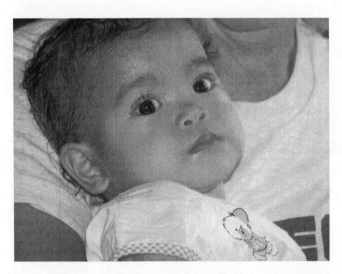

Putri Dua awaiting surgery in the states

The little girl with the heart defect I noted above had appeared at the comms tent one night in the arms of a most remarkable woman, an American nurse named Linley York. I looked up at the sound of Mrs. York's voice. "Is there a doctor here?"

I stood up in the darkness and approached her.

"Hi. I'm Bill McDaniel, and an orthopedic surgeon. What can I do for you?"

"Would you listen to this little girl's heart? She is from the orphanage here on the island."

With some reluctance I donned my stethoscope. A little known fact is that those things hurt your ears! And, especially my ears. Many years of wrestling in high school, college, and the military had left me with the infamous "cauliflower" ears we all tend to get. Perhaps one of the reasons I became an orthopedic surgeon was so that I would seldom have to put those things in my ears. While I did a cardiology elective in medical school and can identify murmurs okay, I still did so with some trepidation.

As I approached the little girl's chest wall with the scope I could hear the murmur well before the scope actually touched her chest. A noisy one, and one that certainly indicated significant structural abnormalities.

"This little girl needs to see a real doctor," I opined. I agreed that we would medevac her to the ship on the next flight. More on her later, because there is a lot more.

Back to the nurse, Linley York. She had dedicated her life to traveling the many, many islands of Indonesia seeking out the poorest of the poor and getting them medical care. She was tireless, and had done this for many years. She begged money from friends and NGO's, got money from her husband's work, but above all, never gave up. As I have come to know her over the last 8 years she has impressed me more than I can ever express. I have been able to help her occasionally in getting institutions here in the States to agree to render care free of charge. However, she still has to raise the money for passports, visas, airline tickets, and arrange for host families where the patients can live while they receive care here in the states. She is truly amazing and represents all that is good about America...and humanity.

While we had been able to get several children from Banda Aceh back to the states for treatment by several means, it usually involved passing the hat around the ship to get the needed funds. (Various hospitals in the states would take care of the medical conditions if we could do the paperwork and legalities needed to get the patients to them, as well as raise the money for expenses other than direct medical care. We did this in a variety of ways, though most involved some element of dipping into our own pockets or asking others to do the same. We were never disappointed.) After the specialists aboard Mercy had determined that the little girl (Putri Dua was her name.) definitely needed surgery, we again began the process of finding some place in the states that would be willing to operate on her. As it turned out UCLA Medical University agreed to do the surgery free of charge if we could get her there. The total cost of all the logistics involved appeared to be about $18,000.00. So, I determined to start sending out pleas to friends stateside for funds.

One of the Project Hope physicians approached me. "Admiral, what are you trying to raise money for now?"

I explained the situation to him.

"May I use your satellite phone? A wealthy friend told me as I was leaving to call him if he could help."

Well, by all means! He called, explained the situation, and disconnected.

"He just wants to know where to send the money."

As I have noted many times before, there are an incredible number of wonderful people in the world, and an extremely significant number of them live in America.

The little girl...who as I have noted was one of the most beautiful babies I had ever seen, was seen and operated upon at UCLA. She is doing fine today, though Linley York told me recently she continues to live at the orphanage on Nias Island. I am amazed that she is still there.

Subject: Sitrep Nias Island 16 April

We continue to function at maximum capacity. There is no letup, nor do I expect any until we leave. There are no clinics running on Nias, only the hospital. I spent last night ashore. During the evening I had 3 doctors from International Medical Corps come up to our comms center and tell me about a total of 7 patients they had brought in from hours away. We discussed the specifics, and by phone the ship agreed to see the patients as soon as possible, and for them to be at the helo field at 0730 this morning for pickup and evaluation and treatment. The doctors sat down with me and talked about what Mercy means to them. And, in these circumstances, Mercy means everything. The female physician sat with tears on her face when she explained, **"You don't know how much it means to us to have you all here. We know you will take care of our people we find. You don't turn us away, and you don't put obstacles up in front of us. You just don't know how much your attitude impresses us. Thank you."**

Shortly before this we had sent our van to pick up an Australian woman working for another of our outstanding partners, AusAid. She had fallen from her moped and had a scalp injury, and they were worried about a skull fracture. She was monitored overnight, and she went to Mercy on the same flight as the patients above. These people risk their lives going into the mountains and finding the sick and injured to bring out to us; they know we are there for them as well.

I came back to Mercy this afternoon, and as I entered our 'fishbowl' (staging area for outgoing personnel), about 10 patients and family were waiting to go back to shore. They all smiled and waved, and several stood up and grasped my hand, touching their hearts. They don't know me. But, they knew that I was part of Mercy.

You have read most of what happened yesterday from other reports. Briefly, AMB Pascoe and Rear Admiral Quinn visited

Mercy, then visited our sites ashore. It was a very successful visit, and the local government officials turned out in force.

Yesterday we had 9 admissions and did 11 surgeries. Our outpatient clinics, especially optometry and dental, did outstanding work, generating numbers similar to below. Today we had 13 admissions and 13 discharges, and did 7 surgeries. We saw a total of 14 consults ashore, examined 205 patients for glasses, dispensed 175 pairs of glasses, and saw 59 dental patients from whom we delivered 170 teeth.

We took our little 2 month old back to shore today, where she died shortly afterward of overwhelming pneumonia. The Chaplain, CDR Commish, and CDR Bangs did outstanding work in dealing with the administrators of the hospital, the decedent affairs department ashore, and finding the mother's family and delivering the mother and child to them with appropriate ceremony. For such a sad event, it could not have gone more smoothly. CDR Bangs especially was very instrumental in helping with the appropriate gestures and events to make this result possible.

Two Project Hope physicians, Dr. Mike Polifka and Dr. Andrew Sutton, go ashore daily and make rounds at the hospital. This is not as simple as it sounds. There are no wards as we know them. Multiple patients per room, a language barrier, everyone wanting to come to Mercy...but we can't take everyone; having to pick and choose who comes and who doesn't, yet be sensitive to turning down patients for transfer. They work extremely hard at this, and are very, very good at what they do. Today they were accompanied by one of our Navy urologists. These doctors are our gatekeepers, and our success would not be possible without them. Saturdays are especially busy for them because none of the local doctors show up, and they have a heavy influx of patients seeking to bypass the local system and get to Mercy. If we had 200 beds staffed, we would fill them.

The Chaplain reported on his comrel efforts. On Monday they will renovate a school library, on Tuesday a nursing school, and on

Wednesday start working on a boarding facility which will take some time.

Preventive medicine had a big day also. They hosted a water management meeting attended by many organizations, such as UNICEF, Oxfam, International Red Cross, and several divisions from Jakarta. Our people had the lead, and will test several more water sources before submitting their final report. Jakarta is already taking action based on their initial results.

They assessed a local hotel where many NGO's stay, and found it safe.

The malaria prevention team had an intense day as they provided training for 30 local and NGO personnel on mosquito eradication. They then provided enough pesticide to last for months, and the teams spread out around the island to begin an intensive mosquito eradication program.

There has been a significant increase in respiratory illness, so they are doing air sample analyses to attempt to determine the cause. The local toilet facilities are very primitive. We have contracted to clean and upgrade them.

Dr. Donald van Nimweg of Project Hope met with the hospital administrators, with CDR Bangs acting as interpreter. They worked out a plan to get passports and visas and permission for the children they wish to return to the States for surgery.

As I have noted before, everyone is working extremely hard, as they have done for several months now. Morale remains high. However, working at this level day after day is incredibly fatiguing. The people on Mercy have the constant stress of dealing with major problems and the need to move them off the ship as quickly as possible to make room for others needing care, and the people ashore are constantly having to deal with the stifling heat while they literally decide who gets to have a chance to live a better life...or perhaps live at all...by coming to Mercy. We have a finite capacity, though we continually strive to push the limits of that capacity, and will never turn down a patient we can truly help.

If there is to be a follow on HA mission after Nias Island, it must be adequately staffed. This outstanding staff, who is giving everything they can give, cannot be asked to do a follow on mission with a skeleton staff. We have heard from many sources that this brand of 'diplomacy' is achieving outstanding results on all fronts; if that is so, and I believe it is, we must have an adequate number of people to be able to continue that record as we go forward.

Bill McDaniel

Sitrep Nias Island 17 April

Very little to report today. This was our first rest day since arriving, and was a no fly day. There were no surgeries performed, and I think all were pleased that we could breathe deeply and relax. The only folks to be a little shook up were on our shore team, which felt quite vividly a 6.2 quake on Nias Island last night. They reported that some degree of earth movement went on for 3 minutes. I'm not sure if that time is accurate, but know from experience that the seconds do stretch out when the ground is moving about under you!

A number of us had the great pleasure of going out in one of the lifeboats for many circuits of Mercy; it was a beautiful day, and a super day for pictures. The Master is exercising the life boats daily when the waters are calm, and the crew is urged to partake, and is doing so eagerly.

All the patients appear to be doing well, with a couple of exceptions in the ICU. We got a 15 year old female medevac patient into the ICU late yesterday; she was riding a moped that was hit by a bus, and our shore crew called for a medevac, wisely. The girl and her father came aboard; she was unconscious, and upon examination had several broken ribs and a hemothorax (one of her lungs full of blood). A chest tube was placed in for drainage, and she is in the ICU doing fairly well at this time.

Our little 13 month old who I held and brought to the ship a week ago is doing fine from his pneumonia, but continues to have occasional seizures. He is being treated for them, and is responding. He likely has a viral encephalitis. The worst case we have is a 2 week old baby who was admitted a few days ago with a fever. Tests show that he has hemorrhagic dengue fever from a mosquito bite. This is a very serious disease in someone this young, and his chances of survival are very small. After the death of our little baby yesterday on shore, the ICU staff, nurses and pediatricians have been grieving a lot over both of these babies. Like they always do, they have put their hearts into the effort to save these kids, and losing any is a blow. While all of us on Mercy take any loss personally, none take it on so personally as those nurses, doctors, and corpsmen who spend day and night with them, fighting their battles to recover with them. We all grieve with them, and support them as we can.

Tomorrow is going to be another busy day, with the usual consultations ashore, many discharges from Mercy, and undoubtedly many admissions to Mercy. The comrel (community relation) teams have a full day planned, as do the PHS (Public Health Service) and Preventive Medicine teams. I will be ashore tomorrow night and will not submit a report until Tuesday, our time.

Bill McDaniel

Sitrep Nias Island 19 April

You have received the numbers from yesterday via Mercy sitrep from the Captain, so I will not go over them much. 13 admissions did stress the staff, however, along with the 13 discharges. Especially in ICU, where the level of intensity continues unabated. Lots and lots of man hours spent there by our ICU staff, most of whom we lose on Friday when Project Hope personnel disembark. 11 surgeries yesterday, and again dental and optometry saw many patients ashore.

There were several interesting encounters ashore yesterday. A 34 year old Indonesian woman came walking up to our comms center with one of the most unusual clinical conditions I have ever seen. 19 years ago she sustained a broken left tibia (shin bone). Two metal plates were wired to the bone at that time as splints, I suppose. Soon the skin and tissues overlying the bone and the plates became infected and the plates and bone were exposed to the air, in a hole in the front of her leg about 3 inches by 2 inches. The bone healed, however, and she had been walking around with this infected wound for 19 years! With metal plates, wires, and bone clearly visible. How in the world she managed to do this is beyond me. When we asked her what bothered her most, she said, "The smell." We looked at her leg and told her we thought we could help her, getting rid of the plates and wire, getting rid of the infection, and covering the bone. As our interpreter explained to her that she would have to go to the ship by helicopter, but everything would be free, etc., she started crying. The helo ride does scare some folks, and some have backed out because of it. We asked why she was crying? **"Because no one has ever offered to help me before."** This sort of brings it back to the reason we are here. Because we can offer to help.

One of our comrel teams was at a school painting and repairing the library. As they began work in the morning, RP2 Bryant, working on the team, noted that the classroom next to the library had no teacher. He found out that the teacher had run off to the mountains after the earthquake on Saturday, and he had not returned to the room of 12-14 year old kids. Bryant stepped into the classroom and took over. Using his Indonesian phrase book, he started teaching the class the English translations. He was writing on the blackboard, the kids were excitedly reciting everything out loud, and he had them singing the "A,B,C" song. They loved it! He spent the entire day teaching, and would occasionally sit at the desk, pound it with his fist, and shout, "Dunia!" ("The World!") The kids would all shout it back in return. I have no idea why he did that, but apparently they did. There was an interested crowd of about 50 envious school kids of other ages watching through the windows as he taught. It was truly amazing, and probably those kids will never forget this impromptu substitute teacher. However, they never did catch on to the concept of "Old McDonald Had a Farm."

We had only 3 admissions today, and 6 discharges; with the intensity level of the patients in the hospital, and with the pending departure of the majority of our nursing staff in 3 days, we had to slow things down a bit. We did 11 surgeries again, however, including the surgery on the young woman noted above. (I scrubbed in and tried to stay out of the way, and I think her wound will heal and the bone will no longer be exposed. The metal plates, 19 years later, looked brand new. Darned good metal.) On shore we saw 10 consults, optometry saw 206 patients and handed out 194 pairs of glasses, and dental, under the leadership of "Quick Hands" CDR Kurt Hummeldorf, saw 98 patients and pulled a total of 251 teeth. Kurt was so tired tonight he had trouble lifting his arms. An interesting vignette occurred in the endless optometry line. A fellow who had been waiting for a few hours to get his turn with the optometrist passed out and had a seizure. Our staff took care of him and attempted to call an ambulance. However, he came to and realized that if he went to the hospital, he would lose his place in line. He refused further care until he got to have his eyes checked. These folks do like their new eye glasses.

Drs Polifka and Garrett handled consults today, and gently started turning down patients whose care is going to take longer than we are going to be here, and whose intensity of care is going to be too high. Thus begins our exit strategy, discussed at length and initiated today. One of the major problems here is going to be the lack of physician medical staff when we leave. There are a number of other volunteer physicians in the hospital, but most will be gone by the time we leave. The hospital is currently staffed with only a couple of general practice doctors. They will have a difficult time. One of the saving graces, however, is that there is a nursing school here, and the nurses wind up staffing the hospital and doing most of the medical work. We are intensifying our efforts to educate the nurses through CDR Suzanne Clark's efforts.

The comrel team got lots of painting done today, and volunteers from the San Jose and Niagra Falls vied to see who could get the most done; they both did great. 30 volunteers worked hard all day, and will continue to work on the nursing school for some time to come.

Preventive medicine and Public Health did 2 major projects today.

First was extensive air sampling, then going into the hospital and instructing the hospital staff on the use of nebulizers and bronchodilators. They have been treating asthma patients with cough syrup, and now have a basis for correct treatment of these patients, who will likely be happy for the effort.

A team went to Lololofuti village today to do structural analyses of the buildings and see if they sustained much damage from the earthquake. They were met at the landing zone by 942 villagers, the entire population. Then, all adjourned to the village elder's home, where that gentlemen noted that our team was the first Westerners in the history of that village to have ever visited there. In fact, immediately after the earthquake the chief had his folks construct their first helicopter landing site, assuming that perhaps there would be teams coming out to check up on things. Today, he was a proud man. His preparations had not been in vain. Once the team had checked out all of the buildings (all were OK), he gathered them together and apologized. Their tradition is to 'share bacon' with distinguished visitors, but they had not had time to kill a pig and cook it. So, he gave them a live pig. They had a problem; a refusal without good reason would insult him. (There admittedly was strong consideration to accepting the pig and returning to Mercy with it just to see what would happen next.) However, they explained to the chief that pigs generally were not allowed on helicopters, and they had to regretfully refuse the gift. They were allowed to leave only after signing a pledge that upon their return someday they would stay long enough to 'share bacon.'

CDR Clark, as noted, taught a class of 55 students today how to start IV's; there was great enthusiasm from the nurses for the project.

Our humanitarian team, including our JAG lawyer, continued to work today at getting two kids needing complex surgery back to the States for care. They met with both the Bupati (sort of a super mayor) and the governor of Sumatra, both of whom strongly support their efforts. They are working closely with the US Embassy as well.

Finally, Mercy's helos and small ship boats continue to do absolutely outstanding work, and all personnel were ashore by 0730 this morning. As has been their standard, CAPT Leahy and his crew are supplying the strongest possible support for our efforts here, and are full members of this team in every way.

Today we returned a 41 year old man to his home where he can die while with his seven children and his wife. He was crushed in the earthquake, and is paralyzed from the mid-chest down. We have been working with him for 2 weeks now, but he just has too many problems, and we cannot save him. We took him and his 17 year old son back to Gunungsitoli Hospital yesterday. Several of us spent most of the day trying to find someone to return him to his village in the mountains about 40 km away. There were no takers. The UN helos are down, and for ambulances it is an all day trip. So, we considered the mission on Mercy and felt that we owed him and his family our best shot at it. Today we placed him in a helo, and the HC-5 pilots went looking for the coordinates. At the site the 'landing zone' was covered with tents. They flew around the village looking and landed in the middle of the very large playground of the local school. (No children were visible.) This was probably the biggest event in the school's history, and classes immediately let out and the children stood on the verandas cheering and waving, closely monitored by their equally cheering teachers. We carried our patient with great care to a local house, where he was to remain while his son walked the 2 km to get some family to help carry his father home. When I returned to the ship tonight I was asked many questions by lots of staff about him, all anxious to hear that we had been successful an reuniting him with his family.

I've noted it before, but it still somewhat stuns us at how appreciative and delightful these people are. It is truly a pleasure to work with them, and for them.

Bill McDaniel

A couple of notes about the above sitrep. While I was helping in surgery with the woman with the chronic infection and exposed plates in her leg, one of the wires which had been in her body for 19 years suddenly came loose and stabbed me in the finger through my gloves. A little bleeding, but after surgery I scrubbed vigorously. As noted earlier, we have no idea of the HIV status of these patients; we consciously chose not to do HIV testing when we arrived in February. Positive results would just confuse everyone, and there was no effective treatment anyway, so we just treated every patient as if they might be positive. I.e., we double gloved and took great care. Except for me, of course. I consulted the infectious disease nurse after surgery. We both agreed that there was little likelihood of serious contamination (at least she agreed; I had my doubts!), so we just watched. I had an HIV test several months later which was luckily negative. Clumsy people probably should not do surgery!

The gentleman we returned to his village had initially been seen by one of our evaluating teams 2 weeks before, 8 days after the earthquake. He had been trapped under the wall of his house which had fallen on him. He lay there for 8 days, surviving somehow, and when pulled out was paralyzed from the waist down. He had an atonic bladder and had not urinated in 8 days, and had renal shutdown. In addition his entire backside was necrosed down to muscle from pressure. We had nothing definitive to offer him and the team initially turned him down for admission. He really needed to go to a chronic care facility…to die. However, there was no such facility for him to go to. I suggested to them that we could at least take him aboard, stabilize him, put an indwelling catheter in, and

184

treat him for his renal failure in hopes it would resolve. We did so, much to his family's relief. However, after finally making him somewhat comfortable, allowing him to have a catheter, and after his kidneys had started functioning again, he was still destined to become septic and die at some point in the near future. You just can't lose 50% of your skin coverage down to muscle and live, especially with no outstanding long term care facilities available. So, we finally took him home where he could be with his family for his remaining time. He seemed happy and resigned to his fate, and his family was delighted. After we moved him from the helo to a local house the helo pilots and I pooled all of the money we had in our pockets and gave to his son. They would need it. A very sad, but oddly quite happy, ending to a tragedy....

Sitrep Nias Island 20 April

Winding down. We start as hard as we can, build up quickly, then immediately start calculating and trying to make sure we get every patient off Mercy before we have to leave. There is nothing constant about this; always changing, adapting to events like suddenly moving Mercy to Sibolga to off-load those of us going home on Friday.

We have contacted most everyone and almost all understand that we have a finite amount of time to spend here, and the end is rapidly approaching. The only ones who do not understand are the patients, who see us as the only decent medical care most of them have a chance of ever receiving. However, while I am sure they do not understand the timing of or reason for our departure, they accept it with a smile, or with sadness—but still with a smile—and go on about their life. They appreciate anything we can do for them. As the young lady with the tibia plates exposed told us, "No one has ever offered to help me before."

I did not go ashore today, but instead spent the day making leisurely rounds and watching the patients. We could still be off Banda Aceh; there is still the support and friendship between all the

185

patients and family members, the easy way of relating to each other and to us, the laughter on Ward 1, where most of the children are. Our little 18 month old girl with the heart defect is certainly one of the most beautiful children I have ever seen, and charms everyone by smiling, laughing, clapping her hands, and delighting in being the center of attention. It does look like we will be able to complete the tedious process of getting her and the 7 year old back to the States for care.

I talked for a long while with a 26 year old interpreter, Ayu, who was also with us in Banda Aceh. She wanted to know which I liked better, Aceh or Nias. Not about to fall into that trap, I praised them both. She laughs easily and is very fluent in English. I asked her about her family. Her Mother, two cousins, and Ayu hopped in their car and tried to outrun the tsunami. Everyone else drowned when the car was inundated. She managed to swim out through a window, and remembers seeing her older brother running carrying her 4 month old cousin. She saw the tsunami catch up to them, and for a moment could see only his arm holding the baby above the water; then it disappeared. She saw the baby and arm one more time, then both went down again. She managed to grab on to a building and saved herself. That night she was going from building to building...and found her brother and 4 month old cousin, miraculously alive. I realize this is old news, but listening to Ayu softly tell it, it will never be old news to her.

Benny, the little baby I held on to and talked to several days ago for a couple of hours while waiting for the helo to arrive, is surviving well. His seizures are controlled, but no one will know for some time if he will have normal mental function. Holding him brought back a flood of memories; I noted that he did squint a little when I was talking with him. I expect he got tired enough of hearing me the last time I talked with him for so long. The young lady whose leg we operated on yesterday is doing well. And, the surgeons did a major surgery yesterday, taking out part of a diseased lung from a young woman, totally changing—and extending considerably—her life. She looks super today. Finally, the 15 year old girl we did emergency surgery on a couple of days ago after she was hit by a bus is looking outstanding, and will be extubated (tube removed from her trachea) soon.

We did 9 surgeries today. We sent 72 people ashore. 10 consults were seen, and optometry saw 172 people and gave out 155 pairs of glasses. Dental saw 45 patients, but upped their average per mouth by taking out 204 teeth. One patient skewed the average, however, by contributing 26 teeth to that total. As has been noted before, none of these patients has ever seen a dentist before—and that one probably won't again. Today was an extremely hot day ashore, and even the locals were seeking shade and shaking their heads.

Three ER doctors from Project Hope went in, Dr. Polifka, Dr. Garrett, and Dr. John Neal, who will be taking over their duties after tomorrow, as he is staying on. They noted that they are seeing very few earthquake related injuries at this time, but lots of major tumors and other chronic problems as people become aware that we are here. Unfortunately, these are all too long term to attempt to treat now. Luckily, 4 or 5 new Indonesian volunteer physicians have shown up to work at Gunungsitoli Hospital; they were badly needed. We are screening now for those cases we can get in and out within a few days, and which have a low grade of acuity, requiring much less nursing care.

The comrel folks under Chaplain Owen had a good day again. They finished painting much of the nursing school, plus patching some floors. They did lots of painting and repairs to the boarding school, and repaired a roof and eaves so that the leaks are now stopped. They installed lighting in one room. A total of 31 folks from 3 ships were in these working parties.

CDR Suzanne Clark continues to upgrade the quality of medical care by teaching the 57 nursing students. Today they learned all about wound care and sepsis. She noted that the hospital has had a ventilator donated, but no one knows how it works. One of our anesthesiologists will go in tomorrow and examine it and teach them how to use it.

The environmental health folks went to the NGO Oxfam and worked with them today. They found an obscure water system serving about 500 people and sampled it for quality, plus taking a number of air samples.

2 preventive medicine and Public Health teams flew to outlying areas. Lowala is a village of 2000 people where they looked at the clinic, churches, and schools, for a total of 19 buildings examined. One of the school buildings, with a total of 300 students, is unsafe. They will get IOM to donate enough tentage to move the kids out of that building.

The other team went to Madrahay village, where another 37 buildings were inspected, including 4 churches, schools, puskesmas (local health clinics), etc. Water samples were taken from the local water supply source, and the local nurse was given training. They donated some medications to the clinic.

Unfortunately, no 'bacon sharing' was offered today.

In our humanitarian mission to get the two children to the States for surgery, LT. Molldren, the JAG lawyer, spent quite a bit of time ashore with Dr. Van Nimweg and CDR Bangs visiting with the Governor and the Bupati. We should have all paper work completed to get the passports and visas tomorrow. Again, CDR Bangs is absolutely invaluable in this effort as he knows the politics of the situation, who to talk to, how to talk to them, and speaks the language. This would be almost impossible without his efforts.

Tomorrow will be a light day as we have a re-supply going on. Friday is a national Indonesian holiday, so we will send in only 30 people as the ship transits to Sibolga and back. Tonight the MSC crew had an ice cream social on the fantail for the Project Hope personnel. (Inasmuch as I needed to report on this event, I attended and had some MSC ice cream as well.) The ship's Master, CAPT Leahy, offered deeply felt thanks to the Project Hope personnel for their part in this last several months' evolution. He noted that this was a most unique undertaking, which it certainly is. No one who has been here will ever forget it, and most of us have grown considerably in our appreciation for our fellow inhabitants of this earth because of being part of these events.

Bill McDaniel

I've mentioned the 14 year old girl with the fractured pelvis we brought on board shortly after we arrived. Her name is Dua, with the hard accent on the "Do." DO-a. I took great delight in greeting her and pronouncing the first syllable softly; she always immediately corrects me. "DO-a!" She has taken over most of the care of the 18 month old little girl, Putri Dua, who is awaiting transfer to UCLA for heart surgery. Putri Dua sits on the bed with Dua most of the day, delightfully playing and charming us all. How will we get along without the presence of these dear and delightful people? They will certainly always be a part of our lives forever; perhaps we will be remembered in theirs as well. Or not. It really makes no difference; we will always remember and love them in our memories..

Sitrep Nias Island 21 April

This will be my final sitrep…for a while at least. The last time I wrote that, I was proven wrong.

Morale continues quite high, but the last several weeks have been intense and tiring. None of the Project Hope people want to leave, but know it is time. They all feel bad about leaving so many seriously ill people on board, especially in ICU, where the load is heaviest.

Again, I think this experiment on at least two fronts has been more successful than anyone could have imagined when we all got together back in late January. The first outstanding success is the melding together of the volunteer Project Hope personnel, Public Health folks, Navy, and Civmars. We truly have fed off of each other's energy and successes, and all have taken great delight and pride in working with each of the other groups named. I will say once again that we need to formalize this working relationship and plan together to meet future contingencies.

The second, and even more meaningful, success we have all seen here is the incredible impact this team, plus USS Abraham Lincoln and the Essex task force have had on public opinion in this part of the world. Instead of coming in and running our operations independently of what other countries were doing, we came in and became a part of everyone's efforts—in support of those efforts. We brought a tremendous force, but did not use it forcibly. The end of this sitrep will hit on this point again. This is diplomacy of a different sort, and clearly a diplomacy effort that works.

There were 5 surgeries performed today. Inasmuch as Mercy is steaming to Sibolga to let many of us off, the work day today was significantly shortened and far fewer people went ashore. We admitted one child who had lost part of 3 fingers. All the patients on Mercy are progressing well, with at the moment only one or two persons we might have to work at getting off the ship on the 29th. There were only 5 consults ashore, and optometry saw 162 patients, giving out 131 pairs of glasses. Dental saw 63, removing 184 teeth.

CDR Clark again took a small team and taught 54 nursing students today. A physical therapy tech went with her and taught crutch walking and how to get patients in and out of bed when they are injured. 10 nursing students are aboard Mercy learning directly from our nurses here.

Our humanitarian transfer of 2 patients to the States for surgery is going well. All the paperwork has been completed and they will visit Sibolga on Friday to get passports and visas.

We are looking at more ways to help support Gunungsitoli Hospital with equipment, supplies, and working with their medical personnel ashore. Several volunteer nursing groups represented by the Project Hope nurses aboard Mercy are looking at adopting the hospital and providing equipment in the future.

The Preventive Medicine and Public Health teams went to Umbillatio today, examining 38 buildings and taking water samples.

We are looking at ways to provide oxygen to Simileu Island, and looking at requested medicines and equipment from the hospital there.

Finally, for this last sitrep, I would like to quote the Curator of the National Museum in Jakarta, Tamilia. She is highly educated and a delightful woman, and spent the last week with us in Banda Aceh aboard Mercy as an interpreter. On her last night aboard she was asked to give a short talk, and below is the spontaneous speech she gave. I think it sums up our impact far better than anything I could add, and is an appropriate and fitting conclusion to this effort.

"I think that it was Sir Arthur Chesterfield who said something along the lines that the human species is happiest when it is of service to others. Well, I do not think that I shall ever be on a happier ship than this one.

You, doctors and nurses who have worked on this ship treating the wounded Acehnese tsunami survivors are extremely special people with an enormous compassion and empathy for others, especially for those who are suffering. You are truly good people - if you were not you would never have volunteered to be on this ship and I think that when a large group of truly good and caring people are collected together in one place like this - it creates a certain energy of its own which has far reaching effects.

I do not know if you are aware of it but when I left Jakarta to join the Mercy the front page article of one the newspapers in Jakarta was about how Indonesian public opinion towards America was taking a major turn. This happened after Indonesians started reading about and watching via the television the thousands of mercy missions flown by the helicopters of the USS Abraham Lincoln off the coast of Aceh. Daily the helicopters dropped food, water and medical supplies to the survivors of the tsunami whom my government would never have been able to reach in time after the enormous destruction of roads, bridges and communications by the tsunami. And later Indonesians witnessed the compassion of the doctors and nurses of the USNS Mercy as they treated over 19,500 Acehnese patients and performed over 250 operations. I do not think that any other government in the world would have been able to provide such an enormous quantity of aid so rapidly because no other government is equipped with the enormous war machine that the United States has and what happened is that in the last three months we have watched that great war machine being used for something totally different and in a way that was completely foreign to us. It was being used to save and heal thousands of lives and quite frankly, at first we Indonesians watched with suspicion and then in puzzlement but finally with gratitude and fondness.

During the last days before the departure of the ship many of the patients were returned to shore to finish their final recuperation at Indonesian hospitals many of which are just starting to fully function again. It was a very emotional time for me as I have had to translate for many of the patients and doctors and nurses as they bid each other farewell. Over and over again this is what the patients have been saying, "I do not know how to thank you. I cannot repay you for what you have done. I have nothing with which to repay you. It is only God who will be able to repay you for what you have done..."

It is one thing to heal people and to give them medical aid but I think that there is another element in all this that you may not be aware of. These people that you have been treating are the poorest of the poor. They eat chicken or meat perhaps once a year. If they eat fish twice a week that is already good. Normally, their meal will be a plate of rice with some chili peppers and a bit of swamp spinach or other vegetable. There has been an insurgency going on here for many years. The military comes and extorts money out of them and burns their houses. Then the separatists come and kidnap them, extort money out of them and burn their houses. They are frequently caught in the cross-fire between the military and the separatists and it doesn't matter because they are just garbage - people of no value. If they go to a hospital for help they are not kept waiting for hours - they are sometimes kept waiting for days and they are treated with arrogance and without care. Indifference is often the best they can expect.

And then they came here. Here you not only healed their bodies but you treated them with such gentleness, such compassion and such great courtesy. For the first time in their lives they were treated as human beings who have worth. You see a man who has lost an arm, a patient who has lost a leg and yet when they leave the ship they are all smiling. The joy in them is overwhelming. They are perhaps happier than they have ever been in their lives because for the first time they are aware of their worth as people - that their thoughts and feelings and lives count. When they leave here they know that they are valuable. They leave with self-esteem. This is something very special and very rare that you have given them.

In Indonesia the words for "thank you" are "terima kasih" which if you translate them literally mean "accept love" for what is it to give someone thanks other than to gave them a part of your love?

So allow me on behalf of my country and my people to express to you our gratitude and to give you our love."

Bill McDaniel

About the Author

REAR ADMIRAL (ret) Bill McDaniel, MD, grew up on a small farm in Oklahoma, attended Oklahoma State University on a wrestling scholarship, then joined the Navy where he remained for 32 years. He is a Viet Nam veteran and had 4 commands in the Navy, one of which was Naval Hospital, Charleston, SC during Hurricane Hugo. He continues to flirt with disaster scenarios to this day, and was instrumental in the U.S. relief effort in Indonesia following the 26 Dec 2004 earthquake and tsunami. He has been married to Shirley for 43 years and has 3 daughters.

www.FacesOfTheTsunami.com